YOU EXHAUST ME

A CLUELESS GUY'S
GUIDE TO MARRIAGE

BOB MARSOCCI

Published by
RAM Publishing

Copyright © 2017 by Bob Marsocci

ISBN: 978-0-69287-518-6

Cover design and typesetting by Gary A. Rosenberg
www.thebookcouple.com

Edited by Carol A. Rosenberg
www.CarolKillmanRosenberg.com

Printed in the United States of America.

To my beautiful wife, Lissette

I've never met anyone like you.
Your perpetual smile and radiant view
of life are infectious.
I love you more today than on the day
we were married.
I am a better person in every possible way
because of you.

*(P.S. Did you ever think that I—of all people—
would write a book giving marital advice?)*

Contents

Marriage (mar`ij). *n.* 1. the state, condition or relationship of being married. 2. the ceremony that formalizes marriage. 3. an intimate association or union. (Source: *Webster's Dictionary*)

Marriage (mar`ij). *n.* 1. the state or condition in which a man relinquishes control and abdicates all decisions to his wife the moment he says, "I do." 2. the ritual that often blindsides men and leaves them perpetually dazed and confused. 3. an intimate union in which no two words are as important as "Yes dear." (Source: *You Exhaust Me: A Clueless Guy's Guide to Marriage*)

"Suddenly, you get married and you're supposed to be this entirely different guy!"

Introduction

I'm going to go out on a limb and guess that if you didn't buy this book, a woman—your girlfriend, fiancée, wife, sister, or perhaps your mother—handed it to you. There's a reason she gave you this book. She believes that you, like I once was, are clueless about what to expect after you say, "I do."

You have no idea that there's such a thing as guest soap that is strictly off limits to you. You don't know the "10 Fatal Words" your wife will say to you in the days leading up to her birthday. You are ignorant about how early on in your marriage you will have to study the "game plan" laid out by your wife for a social event, and you really have no idea why you should pay close attention to gay men when your wife is fraternizing with them.

You are not alone.

Over the years, I've heard many single and/or engaged guys proudly say, "That is never going to happen to me." This usually comes while witnessing a married guy cave in to his wife during a get-together with friends or at some other mixed gathering. Eventually, however, they realize, like most married guys do, they were wrong. Dead wrong.

Once the rings go on, the lovely lady standing across from you wearing white and staring deep into your eyes gains the upper hand. *She* is the boss. *She* calls the shots.

It's a proven (sort of) fact: Over time, husbands give in to their wives on just about everything and anything, no matter how big or small a decision. It just happens. Accept it and learn to live with it. You don't have to take just my word on this somewhat touchy subject. Several years ago, a team of psychologists at the University of Washington studied 130 newlywed couples for six years in an effort to find ways to predict marital success and failure. The study found that marriages that worked well all had one thing in common—the husband was willing to give in to the wife. *Give in to the wife.* In all my years of marriage, this is the sagest advice I have ever heard and I agree with it wholeheartedly.

Have you ever seen a guy propose to his girlfriend between innings at a professional baseball game? The public-address announcer tells fans to direct their attention to the jumbotron and the couple is shown on the enormous screen so everyone in the ballpark can see and hear the proposal. While the guy takes a knee and presents a ring, and the girl starts to cry, have you noticed the distinctly different reactions of the ladies and guys in the crowd? Many ladies cup their hands to their mouth and let out a "ooohhh" sigh. The reaction from the guys? It couldn't be more opposite, as many yell something like "No! Don't do it!" Have you ever wondered why that is? What do these guys allegedly know?

Were it not for what is arguably the most complex,

multidimensional, and mystifying creature (a married woman) to ever grace earth, and the sometimes-sacred institution (marriage) that eventually pulls us unsuspecting guys in like a force field, you would not need this book.

Before I go on, allow me tell you what this book is not about. It's not about me dispensing the type of psychobabble you'll find in all those self-help books written by PhDs on saving your marriage or building a long-lasting one. I am not a psychologist who has spent years studying marriage and/or the opposite sex. I do not travel the country lecturing couples about relationship management. You may be asking, "So who the hell is this guy and what makes him qualified to provide marital advice?" Frankly, I am not in any way professionally qualified to give marital advice. However, I have something I believe is much more valuable: experience. The kind of experience that comes with more than twenty years (and counting) of marriage.

There's no greater qualification than experience, and if you follow my lead, you will benefit from my years in the trenches. I've seen it all. I've climbed Mt. Marriage, made it to the top—albeit having tumbled down its side countless times—and want to guide you and other clueless guys to the peak.

I am an average guy who, before I got married, was absolutely clueless about the nuances and mind-boggling idiosyncrasies that define wives and marriages, and ultimately, for better or worse, how those idiosyncrasies shape the daily behavior, attitudes, thought patterns, and decisions of married men.

Based on my firsthand experience as a once-clueless guy, I wrote this book to tell you my story as a husband —a story laden with lessons learned the hard way. I want you to learn from my mistakes and experiences. How? Well, in *You Exhaust Me* (a title, by the way, that reflects what my wife says to me when I push her to the edge and she no longer wants to deal with me), I provide revealing, helpful, and unconventional guidance about some of the common and not-so-common things you can expect from your wife. I like to think of it as a marriage survival guide for the uninitiated.

I met my wife, Lissette, in 1991. During those twenty-five-plus years, my sister-in-law, Victoria, has always said the same thing to me whenever I try to tell her my side of the story about something I did that landed me in "trouble" with my wife. "Robert," Victoria says before I've even finished, "you get in trouble because you don't think, you don't listen, and you don't pay attention!" She is convinced that I put myself in the day's predicament because I didn't make the effort to think before speaking or listen closely enough to Lissette's comments or pay attention to her subtle (or not so subtle) hints.

You don't think. You don't listen. You don't pay attention. While she makes it sound so simple, I have been struggling to synthesize all three of these seemingly invaluable yet elusive virtues for years. I usually get one of three, so if marriage were baseball, I'd be an all-star player with a .333 average.

While this book offers a humorous and lighthearted look at marriage, it is my hope that the stories I share will honestly help you better understand your wife, your marriage, and ultimately yourself (with regard to your wife and marriage). Based on my decades-long experience as a husband, I want to impart as much knowledge to you as I possibly can in these pages. I hope that you will benefit from my knowledge so that when someone asks you, "How is married life?" you can say without hesitation, "It's awesome!"

Throughout *You Exhaust Me,* I poke fun at my marriage and the common-denominator idiosyncrasies (perhaps even stereotypes) of married women, and although this is a humorous book, I want to make two things clear. First, you may be inclined to make assumptions about my wife because I jest about her actions throughout my book. I want to be clear that she is an amazing wife (she puts up with me), has the kindest soul of anyone I have ever met, and I love her unequivocally. Second, women typically are the glue that holds families and relationships together. They are the steady rudders of the family ship, guiding the family through choppy waters that come along every so often. Most of the married guys I know credit their wives for creating and fostering a well-adjusted and harmonious household.

I have come to greatly admire just about every married woman I know for her innate ability to instinctively know what is best, not for just her immediate and extended family, but for her community and just about any situation or scenario that arises. While a woman's instinct and intuition aren't tangible—they can't be seen or touched—they are as powerful a sense as any. (That's why I have dedicated a chapter to the power of a woman's intuition.)

Furthermore, guys, please appreciate the women in your life. Having grown up in an all-boy household (thus the root of my cluelessness), I was ignorant about many of the things women go through simply because of their gender. Whether it's menstruation, pregnancy, childbirth, breast feeding, menopause, or rudimentary things like waxing, "tweezing," or having to wear makeup and high-heeled shoes, do you think you could deal with half the stuff ladies must deal with? We have it easy compared to them.

Finally, I do want to point out that most of the personal anecdotes I share in this book took place during the first five to ten years of my marriage, when I was absolutely clueless. The second decade of my marriage was, at times, also fraught with hard-learned lessons, but nothing like the first ten. After more than twenty years of marriage, I like to think that I am (for the most part) no longer as clueless as I once was. My wife somewhat disagrees. When I told her I was writing this book to give clueless guys marital advice based on everything I've learned as her husband, she paused a beat, looked at me with a slight curve to her lips, and said, "Okay . . . that's great . . . but who says you're done learning?"

1.

Her Birthday: Beware of the 10 Fatal Words

"The best way to remember your wife's
birthday is to forget it once."

—E. JOSEPH COSSMAN

Marriage can be—and quite often is—a beautiful and sacred institution. When you both say, "I do," you get a partner for life (hopefully). You and your wife can enjoy a wonderfully rewarding life of marital bliss, and if you're like most couples, once kids come along, you have something you cherish far more than anything else: your children and your family.

Beautiful picture, right? You found your soul mate, the love of your life, and it's all sunshine and roses. Pump your brakes just a bit, pal. Look, I'm not going to bullshit you: marriage can be beautiful, but it also can be hard—at times, very hard.

I don't care if you have an MBA from Harvard or a PhD from Stanford. You may be the next celebrity astrophysicist or a member of Mensa, but this I can guarantee: no matter how smart you are, you never have and never will encounter anything as complex as your lovely wife and as mind-baffling as marriage. Even Elon Musk, the genius behind Tesla, PayPal, and SpaceX, and arguably the most brilliant man in the world, is twice divorced. He's figured out how to build all-electric cars from the ground up and how to put people on Mars, but he just can't figure out women and marriage.

I think marriage is antithetical to how we treat every other meaningful relationship in our lives. Think about it—could you live with your parents or siblings until "death do you part"? What about living with a close friend or college roommate or your kids for potentially fifty or more years? Could you do that? I know I couldn't. But society, as well as religious and cultural norms, tell (or convince) us that when we get married, we are to live with that person for the rest of our lives.

There is no creature on earth more unpredictable and complex than a wife. Being book smart (or, for that matter, street-smart) has absolutely *nothing* to do with truly understanding what makes your wife tick or the myriad idiosyncrasies and nuances that are inherent with every marriage. Bestselling author and relationship counselor, John Gray says men are from Mars and women are from Venus. Who am I to contradict Mr. Gray? But be that as it may, there are going to be days when you think you and your wife are from entirely different galaxies—forget Mars and Venus.

While marriage can be quite challenging at times, I am going to keep it simple and begin by explaining it in terms that you and virtually every guy (at least guys in the good old U.S. of A.) can understand. Marriage, believe it or not, is a lot like football. You're surprised, aren't you? Both marriage and football require hard work, commitment, sacrifice, dedication, and teamwork. A husband-and-wife team, just like a football team, has its high points and low points. There are days of absolute joy and days of discontent. There are days when everything clicks and goes your way, and there are days when everything, and I mean *everything,* goes wrong regardless of what you say or do.

You're with me so far, right? Good, because here's where it starts to get tricky. There's one big difference between the football gridiron and the domestic playing field known as marriage. Unlike a traditional football game where the teams rotate between defense and offense, as a husband, you are *always* on defense. Get that through your head right now and learn to live with it. You are *never* on offense, and in this league, there are no interceptions or fumble recoveries by you, the defensive unit.

Your wife, on the other hand, is constantly on offense—a high-powered, multifaceted offense—and she is the unflappable quarterback calling all the plays. She is the team captain. She is the team leader. Furthermore, if your wife commits a penalty, it is always reviewed, and the figurative officials always overturn her infractions. (I guess now would be a good time to let you know that your wife also oversees and can overrule the officiating crew.) Your penalties, however, are never overturned—basically, even if you're right, you're wrong. This is not a level playing field.

To better help you understand the new world you will be entering (or have already entered), I am going to clue you in on one of the biggest trick plays that your lovely wife will intentionally put in her game plan that is basically her equivalent of a double reverse play. Just when you think she's going in one direction, she reverses field and goes the opposite way. You, the hapless defender, are running around aimlessly, confused as hell over what to do.

That's not where the similarities between football and marriage end. If there is one vital thing (and sadly there is not just one thing) you need to know as you prepare for your life of wedded bliss, it's this: A married woman's birthday is a man's equivalent of Super Bowl Sunday. If you disappoint your wife on this, *her most special day of the year,* there will be hell to pay. The popular proverb, "Hell hath no fury like a woman scorned," could easily be amended to, "Hell hath no fury like a woman whose idiotic husband screwed up her birthday." Believe me, I have firsthand experience in this dubious area.

Your wife's birthday is very special to her. In fact, to her, it's a holiday just like Christmas or Valentine's Day (aka Extortion Day). Despite what she may tell you, your wife is expecting something special from you on her birthday.

Now pay close attention: *special* to your wife doesn't necessarily mean you have to buy her an expensive gift that will set you back two months' pay (of course, that doesn't hurt). On the contrary, to your wife *special* means that you put some thought behind getting her an original gift or planning something truly memorable for her big day that makes it abundantly clear that you love her and know what makes her happy. She wants you to show her that you know what gets her heart all aflutter.

You've heard the expression, "It's the thought that counts." Well, for your wife's birthday, you better do your best Aristotle impression and put a hell of a lot of thought into what you are going to do or get her for her birthday.

What's the imagery that pops into your head when you think about birthdays? Perhaps it's a surprise party or dinner with friends at a favorite restaurant (helpful hint: do not take your wife to a birthday dinner at a restaurant that has an all-you-can-eat buffet or serves chicken in a bucket).

Birthdays are all about blowing out candles, eating cake, having some drinks, and giving (or receiving) cool gifts. Married women, on the other hand, have at times taken this centuries-old custom and seemingly innocent concept and added a new and potentially lethal twist— in many ways, it's like a sting operation and you are the unsuspecting mark.

Nearly every married guy I know has, at one time or another, heard the same 10 Fatal Words from their wives that can lead to disaster on their birthdays. While the 10 Fatal Words that your wife will spring on you may at first seem innocuous enough, they are part of a well-calculated and premeditated ploy. It's almost like you are being set up by your wife to fail. She doesn't want you to fail—she really wants you to be shrewd enough to see through her little ruse.

The 10 Fatal Words that your wife will say to you in the days leading up to her birthday are: "You don't have to get me anything for my birthday." These 10 Fatal Words are a lit match dangling over a puddle of gasoline, and if you're not careful with how you proceed, you could ignite a four-alarm fire.

When you first hear those 10 Fatal Words from your wife, don't just brush it off as you would if she asked you to watch an episode of *The Real Housewives of Wherever*. In fact, when you hear the 10 Fatal Words, immediately picture above your wife's head a large sign with bright, blinking neon letters that reads: WARNING: THIS IS A TEST AND IF YOU FAIL THIS TEST YOU WILL LIVE TO REGRET IT. I fell for it, and several friends of mine have failed this test as well, making our wives' birthdays memorable for all the wrong reasons.

Translated, "You don't have to get me anything for my birthday," means "You better surprise me with a gift that shows me that you put some thought into it and will make me feel special." Your wife is saying to herself, "You should know me well enough by now to make the extra effort to do something creative and thoughtful for my birthday." She's also thinking, "I want to be inspired and motivated and surprised and genuinely moved by your gift." She wants to cherish the moment. So, for perhaps the first time in your life, you are going to have to buy a gift and/or plan something for someone based not only on the premise that you think she will enjoy it but also on your ability to make it abundantly clear to her that you know what makes her tick. This can be a hell of a challenge.

Furthermore, when a woman receives a gift from her husband (and this isn't limited to just birthdays), she wants something akin to bragging rights. Many of my married friends have reported this, so although my wife thankfully doesn't fall into this subcategory, I felt the need to share it with you. There's a good chance your wife will want to show and/or tell her girlfriends about the gift she received from you and how you made her birthday unforgettable. She will want to make it perfectly clear to her friends that you, her adoring husband, are a thoughtful, considerate, caring, and attentive spouse. After her birthday, one of the first things your wife will probably hear from her girlfriends is, "What did [your name here] get you for your birthday?" She will want to impress her friends, and frankly, some women will even want to make their friends a little jealous. The pressure is on both you *and her,* so you better deliver.

Year one of our marriage was when I first heard the 10 Fatal Words from my wife. I took them literally and responded with, "Really? Okay." *Wrong answer.* I eventually learned that when my wife tells me to not get her anything for her birthday, it's sort of like (hell, it is) reverse psychology.

The 10 Fatal Words are a well-calculated test, and your wife will likely spring the 10 Fatal Words on you when you are most vulnerable and have your guard down, such as when you are glued to the TV during a football game tracking your fantasy team and nothing else exists in your world at that moment.

As far as you're concerned, you know that while you're fixated on a game, there's really no difference between your wife saying, "You don't have to get me anything for my birthday," and "Honey, I just emptied the checking account and I'm going to the Mercedes dealership to buy that new S-Class I've had my eye on." Whatever she says very quickly goes in one ear and out the other while you give the obligatory, "Yeah sure," answer without taking your eyes off the game in progress. While she's telling you to not get her anything for her birthday, your wife will have on her best poker face, but in reality, she's holding four aces. Don't fall for her bluff.

As I admitted above, when I was a rookie husband, I fell for the bluff. I showed up empty-handed on my wife's big day (but at least I had a birthday card). She opened the card, read it, and said in a monotone voice, "Thanks."

Sensing something awry, I said, "What's wrong?"

Like a lot of women, my wife can be very sensitive and teeming with emotion. Even though she said, "Nothing's wrong," I knew I was in for one of her more emotional moments. It was right about then that I noticed the combination of sheer disappointment and deep disgust on her face. So I came back with the obvious, "But you told me to not get you anything for your birthday." Believe me when I tell you, my idiotic excuse made a bad situation even worse.

Lissette replied, "You're not supposed to listen to

me," which frankly contradicted everything she had ever told me.

Digging myself into an even deeper hole, I said, "Then why did you tell me to not get you anything?" (The point was moot and the harm I caused by showing up without a gift was irreparable.)

In response to my feeble defense, my wife said, "Just forget about it . . . you've already ruined my birthday week."*

Of course with my wife visibly sullen—as a result of my actions—on what was supposed to be her special day, it made it pretty damn hard to forget. After what seemed like an eternity, I apologized for about the eighth time for being so thoughtless and insensitive. I tried to make it up to Lissette and took her to her favorite store that day and told her to "Get anything you want. It's on me." While she took me up on my offer, the real damage had already been done, and I had to wait 365 days to really make it up to her.

By the way, with my wife, and I imagine with many married women, a gift certificate to one of her favorite stores doesn't cut it. I've tried that, and in her words, "A gift certificate shows no original thought." Remember, when you get a gift for your wife, most of the time you'll score more points for originality and thought than cost.

The Catch 22 with coming up with a sensational and creative birthday gift for your wife is that you set a

---

*My wife—and expect the same thing from your wife—doesn't have just a birthday, she has a *birthday week*.

level of expectation in her mind that you have to meet, or more likely exceed, year after year. You have raised the bar, so to speak. Let's say you take your wife on a romantic picnic for her birthday this year and she is just giddy that you spent the time and effort to plan something truly special for her. Well, for about 300 of the next 364 days, she is going to be thinking about how you will top that for her next birthday. You're basically damned if you do and damned if you don't.

You probably have already figured this out, but if not, the 10 Fatal Words rule also applies to other special days that come just once a year such as your wedding anniversary (don't forget the date), Christmas, and, of course, Valentine's Day. One Christmas several years ago, my wife's exact words to me in the days leading up to the holiday were, "Let's not exchange any gifts with each other this year."

What was Lissette's idea of not exchanging any gifts? On Christmas Day, she gave me three gifts. I wasn't stupid enough to fall for her ruse, and by sheer coincidence, I got three gifts for her that year.

Go the extra mile on your wife's birthday. Be original. Be creative. Be spontaneous (your wife will love that). Surprise her. Bottom line: when it comes to your wife's birthday get her a meaningful and original gift that she will remember for the rest of her life.

You've heard it before: if she's happy, you'll be happy.

2.

It's Not Always About You

"Bachelors have consciences,
married men have wives."

—H. L. MENCKEN

Assuming you had one, I'm sure you have fond memories of your first bachelor pad that you shared with some friends. It may not have been the cleanest place or had the nicest furniture, but it was your abode and you could come and go and do pretty much as you damn well pleased. Your roommates likely only cared if you paid your share of the rent on time and regularly contributed to the supply of beer.

When you were single and living with other guys, you could come home, throw a steak on the grill, turn on ESPN, and eat your dinner in front of your room-mates without offering them a bite, or frankly, barely acknowledging their presence beyond saying something like, "Hey." And the best part was, they didn't care if you "ignored" them and didn't engage in conversation.

As a guy who likely has spent many years primarily in the company of other guys, inherently you tend to be selfish (I know when I was single I could be selfish, and if you ask my wife she would say I sometimes still am). Don't deny it. Like a living organism, your selfish behavior spawned from a natural environment populated by other single guys who, for all intents and purposes, were just like you. It's not your fault that you were selfish, and I'm not saying this to condemn or stereotype our gender as a group of Neanderthals. I'm also not saying that men don't have altruistic virtues and admirable character traits.

All I'm saying is before you got serious with and/or moved in with a woman, it's likely you spent most of your free time with your guy friends and you naturally became acclimated to guy attitudes. You became a product of your environment, and guy attitudes can be summed up in four words: don't worry about it.

Because your buddies, who were also somewhat selfish, didn't care if you didn't share the intimate details of your day with them, naturally, you didn't care. Years ago, the National Marriage Project (an organization at Rutgers University) acknowledged that single men essentially are cavemen. In a report titled "The State of Our Unions," the authors wrote, "While it is acceptable for single men to be self-indulgent and carefree, it is not so for married men. Once married, men are supposed to work and care for others." In other words, welcome to adulthood.

Here was my so-called prevailing ecosystem/environment before I met my wife: I grew up in a household with three brothers, our father, and doting mother. In college, I lived in a fraternity with about forty guys, and after graduation I had, for several years, the proverbial bachelor pad with three guys as roommates. In all those years of living with other guys, one thing became abundantly clear to me: while single guys may be self-indulgent and self-centered, they also let things slide.

If I didn't offer my roommates some of my dinner, they didn't care. If I planned something for the weekend and didn't include my friends, again, it was no big deal. They really didn't care if I did something that would be considered selfish, and never, in thirty years of bachelorhood, did one of my friends say to me, "You know, it's not always about you," or "I can't believe you didn't think of me." While we occasionally had disagreements, we quickly got over them, and I've never had a friend who held a grudge. As you can surmise, I became all too accustomed to this pervasive cavalier attitude that is inherent in such a testosterone-filled environment.

Fast-forward to marriage, and suddenly I am living with the exact opposite of my roommates—someone who *does* care about what I say and do (or don't say and don't do). I needed to evolve quickly. No longer could I be the self-indulgent person I supposedly was.

I got married, and in my role as a husband, I am expected to be sharing, thoughtful, attentive, more considerate, sensitive, and (this was probably the toughest part) mature and selfless. I clearly remember when I got the "It's not always about you" wake-up call from my wife. It was during our first year of marriage (well before kids), and it was an indelible moment that has shaped the way I now behave on a daily basis.

Before the Internet and iPad put newspapers on life support, one of my favorite things to do on a Saturday morning was to sit down with the *Los Angeles Times* and read the sports section. One particular morning, my wife was already up and I went into the kitchen, said good morning to her, poured myself a bowl of cereal, and sat down at the table across from her with my newspaper.

Just when I was about to look at the latest NBA and NFL standings, Lissette said something like, "You know, did you ever think that I might want some cereal, too?"

Of course, my response was, "Oh, you want some?"

And her response was, "That's not the point."

I said, "What's the point?"

She said, "The point is that you never take time to ask me if I want something that you're having. You should think about me and offer some cereal to me so I don't always have to ask. You really should be more considerate of me. You know, it's not *always* just about you."

I just sat there staring at my cereal bowl as my Cheerios got soggy and didn't know what to say. While physically I was living with my wife, mentally I was still living with my buddies. I eventually apologized to Lissette for not thinking of her and told her I would try to do a better job of being more considerate going forward.

In the twenty-plus years I've been married, I have found that the "It's not always about you" mantra from my wife also applies to dozens of other areas such as grocery shopping, choosing a movie or restaurant, selecting vacation destinations, and, of course, deciding what to watch on TV (thank God—or actually TiVo—for the invention of the DVR).

The irony with the cereal incident was that Lissette didn't actually want any cereal. What she wanted (and still wants) was for me to make the effort to think about her, show her that I care, and not act like the selfish man that I was and sometimes can still be.

A few years ago, a friend and I went to the Palm Springs area with a group to spend the day at the BMW Performance Driving School. We shared a room for one night, and first thing the next morning, my friend said he was heading to the hotel gym. I said, "Okay, I'll probably see you there." As he opened the door to leave our room, he stopped, turned, and said, "You know, if I was with my wife, she probably would have said something like 'Instead of working out, did you ever stop to think that I might want us to go to breakfast or take a walk around the grounds together'?" He, too, is a seasoned veteran of "It's not always about you."

"It's not always about you" is also a euphemism for sacrifice. Marriage, you may have heard, is all about sacrifice. Did you know that the summer of 2017 marks the thirtieth anniversary of the hit film *Dirty Dancing*? Of course you didn't. The only reason I know is because my wife told me it is, and she bought tickets for our family to see the movie on the big screen at a historic theater in Los Angeles. A promo for the anniversary showing says, "Come dressed up in character and make sure you wear your dancing shoes!" This, my friend, is a crystal clear example of the sacrifices married men make. As a Red Sox fan, I do know 2017 is the ten-year anniversary of the Sox winning their second of three World Series titles in a decade. Imagine if I said to my wife, "Honey, I have a great idea—to celebrate the ten-year anniversary of the Red Sox 2007 World Series title, I'm going to order David Ortiz jerseys for you, me, and the girls. We can all go out dressed like Big Papi." That's just not going to happen.

When you get married, you will find that your wife will want you to reach out to her like you've never reached out to anyone else before. Even some of the littlest of things that you think don't matter to her do matter (often, a lot), and if you have a lapse or regress back to your single days, it could trigger a very unpleasant response from her.

So if you want to preempt the "It's not always about you" comment from your wife, don't wait for her to blindside you—the next time you serve yourself a bowl of cereal be sure to ask your wife if she wants a bowl as well.

3.

Her Bag of Bags

"It's a woman's business to get married
as soon as possible, and a man's to
keep unmarried as long as he can."
—GEORGE BERNARD SHAW

In the small front hallway closet of the apartment my wife and I lived in when we were newlyweds, we kept the usual items you would expect to find in a closet, such as jackets, umbrellas, briefcases, and an assortment of hats.

However, there was one thing that I previously never knew existed and certainly didn't expect to find in the closet: a bag of bags. I'm not talking about a paper grocery bag filled with small plastic grocery bags—even my mom had one of those. I'm talking about a big bag filled with other bags of various sizes, materials, and colors that are adorned with haute brand names such as Tiffany, Cole Haan, Louis Vuitton, Coach, and Godiva Chocolate. The plastic bags from Target aren't allowed in this neighborhood.

You see, what you have to realize is this: it's not enough for ladies to have just the extremely overpriced

Louis Vuitton purse. They just can't bring themselves to part with the bag they carried the purse in when they left the store.

My wife, like virtually every married woman, at one time or another, kept a collection of these bags. I've realized that most women collect such bags with the same pride that little girls collect dolls.

As of this writing, I am fifty-two years old and have never kept one bag that would be considered a must-keep bag by most wives. I mean, why on earth would I have held on to such bags? It's just not natural for a guy to do something like that.

Just try to imagine my buddies' reaction if I showed up for a round of golf with my bottle of Gatorade in an aqua-blue Tiffany bag. After laughing their collective asses off, they would make me tee off from the women's tee box.

One day while I was putting some stuff in the closet (which was tiny by today's standards), I happened to innocently stumble across Lissette's prized bag of bags. I didn't know she was collecting them, and I saw that the mother bag was taking up a good amount of space, so I did what any clueless husband would do: I took the mother bag with all the little baby bags and tossed it into the dumpster behind our apartment building. We had plenty of paper and plastic bags from the grocery story, so I figured we certainly didn't need the other bags.

Wrong.

A couple of days later, I was out back washing my car and my clearly distraught wife came outside to ask me what had happened to her bag of bags, and I told her that I removed it.

"You did what!?" she asked incredulously. (It was one of those indelible marriage moments.)

Seeing that I was on the verge of getting into big-time trouble, I told Lissette that we needed more storage space in the closet and that the bag of bags was taking up valuable space. That didn't resonate with her.

"Where are they?" she asked.

I pointed to the dumpster, and that's when she lost it. "I can't believe you did that," she said. "Why? What on earth possessed you to throw away my bags?"

I said, "Um . . . " and she said, "Just forget about it" and stomped back inside the apartment.

Given that she was royally pissed off at me, it was awfully difficult for me to forget about it. About a half hour later, I mustered up the courage to go inside and asked her why the bag was so special, and that's when she explained the importance of a bag of bags.

Women use these bags for, among other things, lunch bags for work, and they also often use them to carry things, such as makeup. I apologized for tossing her bag of bags in the garbage and told her that I'm sure her sister and mother had some bags they could spare until she could replenish her supply. She didn't see the humor in my comment.

Years ago, during a discussion of the bag of bags, a friend told me that his wife was so obsessed with harboring a bag of prized little bags that every now and then he would toss some of the little bags in the garbage while she slept. He'd just reach down to the bottom of the large bag and grab a handful of smaller bags. He figured the small bags on the bottom were the oldest and likely wouldn't be missed. Of course he wouldn't dare toss the larger bag.

Lissette can't stand to see such bags go to waste. On one of our visits to my parents in Rhode Island, Lissette went shopping in Newport at several boutiques. When we got back to my parents' house, she took out the various clothing items she bought to show my mom and then offered the bags from the stores to her. My mom happily accepted her offer and added the boutique bags to her collection. They bonded over bags.

If your girlfriend or wife is like most women, she cherishes her bag of bags. So, I tell you all of this to provide this warning: Don't mess with it. If you happen to notice a rather large bag of bags in the back of a closet while you are innocently putting something away, step away from the bags and close the door. Over time, this bag of bags will grow like a weed, but this is one weed you *do not* want to destroy.

4.

Do You Really Want to Know What I'm Thinking About?

"I haven't spoken to my wife in years.
I didn't want to interrupt her."
—RODNEY DANGERFIELD

One of my wife's and my favorite local spots in Southern California is Laguna Beach, a picturesque seaside town in Orange County. It's about a forty-minute drive from our home to Laguna Beach, and we make the short drive there a few times a year with our daughters to enjoy the scenery, restaurants, and, of course, the beach.

There are spectacular cliffs in Laguna Beach that hug the coastline and are more than a thousand feet above the ocean, and there's also a long walkway that winds up and down the cliff side that provides amazing views of Laguna and the Pacific Ocean. Laguna Beach really is a picture postcard town.

One late summer evening early in our marriage,

my wife and I were strolling along the cliff walk, and we stopped to sit down on the grass to enjoy a fabulous sunset. As we sat there holding hands, the sun was setting over the Pacific and the clouds on the horizon turned burnt orange.

The late actor Dennis Farina had a great line about Southern California sunsets in the movie *Get Shorty:* "They say the fucking smog is the fucking reason why you have such beautiful fucking sunsets." Well, it must have been awfully bleeping smoggy that day because it was one of those beautiful bleeping Southern California sunsets.

After a few minutes of us both silently taking in the sunset, Lissette turned to me and asked, "What are you thinking about?"

I asked her, "Right now?" and she said "Right now."

If memory serves me correctly, at that time, I was thinking about several things: which pitcher was starting for the Red Sox that night, how the Patriots were shaping up for the upcoming football season, and where we were going to eat dinner because I was getting hungry. (A comedian I saw years ago said that wives shouldn't ask their husbands what they're thinking about unless they are prepared to discuss such topics as the shotgun formation, March Madness, and fantasy football.)

Anyway, back to the sunset. I was certain that what I was thinking about during this very romantic sunset was not what my wife wanted to hear from me. Here we were sharing a precious and intimate moment, so how could I possibly tell her that I was thinking about baseball, football, and food? I knew that Lissette would have gone ballistic had I told her what I was really thinking about. Talk about completely ruining the moment.

If Lissette was a sports fan, maybe—and it's a huge maybe—I could have gotten away with telling her the truth. But my wife never has been, and never will be, a sports fan.

Case in point: I have a vintage photo of Ted Williams, the greatest hitter to ever play professional baseball. When I first got the photo, I showed it to Lissette (she had never heard of Williams) and told her that Teddy Ballgame was the last player in Major League Baseball to hit over .400 for a season. Her response to me was, "Four hundred what?" You think I'm kidding? She once told a friend how I was lucky enough to go to opening day at Fenway Park in 2005 to see the "Red Sox get their Super Bowl rings."

So, there we were on the scenic cliff walk and I was put on the spot with the "What are you thinking about?" question. Being quick on my feet, and to buy some time, I said to her, "You tell me first." In addition to being deeply emotional, my wife is a pretty philosophical person so I knew she would say something fairly profound. True to form, she said, "Oh . . . I was just thinking of how lucky and blessed we are to have each other and to be sharing this truly special moment together."

Now, it was my turn, and while I can't remember exactly what I said to her, it was something like,

"You're right. We are lucky to be sharing this time together." She then hugged me and we watched the sun drop into the ocean. About thirty seconds later I said, "Can we go eat dinner now?"

If you haven't experienced something like this yet, just be aware that the "What are you thinking about?" question is inevitable. You are going to get this question from your wife a lot—it's the opposite end of the spectrum that you experienced with your buddies. Think about it. When was the last time one of your buddies asked you, "What are you thinking about?" Never. The only thing that comes even remotely close is when a friend asks you something like, "What game do you want to watch this weekend?" or "Any particular beer you want me to bring over?" While it may take some thought, there are finite options that you already know.

The question doesn't necessarily have to come up just while you and your wife are watching a sunset like in my example or during some other "profound" experience; your wife will want to know what you are thinking about at seemingly random times. She will want you to share your thoughts with her the way you share popcorn with her at the movie theater.

You could be enjoying a rib-eye steak on a Saturday afternoon in your backyard and from out of nowhere, the "What are you thinking about?" question surfaces. Boom! You are blindsided and suddenly your wife, who is sitting across the table from you, wants an answer, and not just some trivial answer.

You can't say something like, "How good this steak

and beer are." She just won't accept that. In between bites of that delicious steak, you have to come up with an answer that has to have meaning and perhaps even be a bit profound and reflective.

To her, the proper answer is, "I'm sorry if I've been pensive, dear. I was just reflecting on what a warm, wonderful, thoughtful, caring, intelligent woman you are, and how lucky I am to have met you." Of course, it's likely you will never come close to saying anything remotely like that.

I think our wives want to know what we are thinking about because, on any given day, they will do the majority of talking between us. Given that your wife is doing the lion's share of the talking, she probably thinks you've absorbed everything she's said and you're in deep thought contemplating and internalizing all that she's sharing with you.

Let's say your wife brings up ten different topics (and that's being conservative) with you during lunch or dinner. Chances are, your ability to retain all that she said is about the same as Shaquille O'Neal's career free-throw-shooting percentage. Like Shaq, who over a nineteen-year NBA career shot 52 percent from the charity stripe, you'll be lucky if you remember half of what your wife shares with you.

The actress Regina Hall summed up this whole "What are you thinking about?" question in an interview with *Esquire* magazine when she said, "You may consider a root canal less painful, but this much is true no matter the woman: We sincerely want to talk (with you) about what you're thinking and how you feel."

So, when you hear, "What are you thinking about?" even if you are thinking about sports and food (and this should be obvious), do not tell your wife that's what you are thinking about, especially if it's during a tender moment. I'm not telling you to lie to her; just consider her feelings and how she will react if you tell her you're thinking about sports and food. Try to be like an NFL quarterback who quickly calls an audible at the line of scrimmage and comes up with a new play on the spot. Your "new play" will be a sincere response. So be creative and try your hardest to tell your wife something profound, meaningful, and deep. Believe me, she will appreciate it.

5

Say What You Mean/ Mean What You Say

"Marriage is all about trust and understanding.
She doesn't trust me and I don't understand her."

—ANONYMOUS

Although my wife was born and raised in the greater Los Angeles area, my in-laws, who are from Guatemala, spoke only Spanish with her when she was a child. Lissette learned to speak English when she went to grade school, but to this day, when my wife speaks with her parents, they primarily speak Spanish.

In the more than twenty-five years I have known my wife and her family, I have been able to pick up various Spanish words, phrases, and expressions just from listening to their conversations. While I'm nowhere near fluent in Spanish, when I meet a Hispanic person who does not speak English, I can hold my own in a conversation—albeit a brief one.

Understanding Spanish is a breeze for me compared to understanding what arguably is the most difficult foreign language for me, or any other married man for that matter, to understand and learn: the secret language of married women. The language of married women is spoken in a top-secret code that not even John Nash, Russell Crowe's character in the Academy Award–winning film *A Beautiful Mind* could crack.

It's as if all wives went to the same clandestine linguistics school.

Nowhere will your wife exercise this secret language more than when you argue with her. You will quickly find that when you're arguing with your wife and she is in the middle of a ten-minute diatribe aimed directly at you, you may think you clearly understand what you just heard and believe that you have correctly interpreted her rant. However, there is a surreptitious meaning to nearly every word coming out of her mouth, and soon you will be left dazed and confused and scratching your head.

Before I delve a little deeper into trying to help you understand this secret language, let me give you some sage advice about getting into an argument with her: Don't. Just don't.

Trying to win an argument with your wife is as futile as trying to make your beer-chugging Irish friend the designated driver on St. Patrick's Day. You're in a no-win situation. It's like David (you) going up against Goliath (your wife), but now Goliath has a bazooka, is locked and loaded, and has dead aim on David with his puny slingshot. This is not a fair fight.

We've all heard the expression, "Never argue with a woman." That phrase really should be modified to, "At all costs—take it to your grave if you have to—never argue with a woman." I have found from my own painful experience that women, unlike men, have a natural and inherent inclination for being very adept at arguing and proving their point. They are very good—some would say exceptional—at arguing. When God passed out arguing skills, men weren't even in the line.

Think of arguing with your wife as similar to gambling in Las Vegas. You know how in Vegas the House always wins? Well, when it comes to arguing with your wife, she is the House and you're the chump who keeps throwing $100 chips down on the blackjack table after you've already been taken to the cleaners. You keep telling yourself, *I can't lose all the time. Eventually I'm going to win.* No, you're not. Give it up. Stand up and walk away from the table.

On his national sports-radio talk show, *The Herd,* Colin Cowherd once succinctly explained to his co-host Kristine Leahy (who is single) the path most married guys take when arguing with their wives. Leahy asked Cowherd if he yells back at his wife when she yells at him while arguing. His response: "There's no point." From his many years of experience as a husband, he knows he is in a no-win situation.

Like all married couples, Lissette and I have had our fair share of verbal spats. I'm a fairly articulate person, but when it comes to verbal sparring with my wife, I eventually become a babbling idiot. It's not that I don't know what to say; it's that when we argue, she succinctly and articulately explains to me her side of the story/point of view, and when she does, it makes my side of the story/point of view seem absolutely inept by comparison.

My wife strikes down my attempt to rationalize or defend my often-misguided words or actions with the deft precision of a UFC fighter throwing a quick and powerful left-right combination. When I argue with my wife, I feel like I'm an amateur fighter who has just stepped into the ring to take on Conor McGregor. Pound for pound, my wife is the best in the world at succinctly making her point. She gives me a quick jab to the head followed by an uppercut to my chin, and I'm down for the 10-count before we make it to the third round. I just got my ass kicked. Again.

I rationalize and my wife reasons. I come up with excuses, and she comes up with facts. Our arguments usually end when one of us (that would be me) says, "Okay, I'm sorry. As usual, you are right," and Lissette says something like, "Now do you understand why what you did was wrong?" or "How would you like it if I did something that stupid?" If I try to get the last word in on an argument, it's not the end of that argument; it's the beginning of a new argument that she ultimately wins.

Lissette also pulls the equivalent of a pop quiz on me when we're arguing. During the middle of an argument, she will say, "Tell me why I'm mad at you." She may be mad as hell at me and she may have spent ten minutes telling me why she's upset with me and what I did wrong, but she wants—no, *needs*—me to tell her why she's mad at me, and try as I might, I can't get away with saying something like, "You just told me why you're mad at me." Of course, she knows exactly why she's mad at me. The point here is that she wants to make sure that I know why she's mad at me and she wants me to tell her. I can pretty much guarantee that your wife will pull the same pop quiz on you during an argument. When your wife gives you the same pop quiz, my advice is to fess up and tell her exactly what she wants to hear.

At times when I argue with my wife, I feel like one of the *Brady Bunch* boys. You may remember when Mr. Brady would, in virtually every episode, ask Greg, Peter, or Bobby, "What lesson did you learn?" after one of them screwed up. With every argument I have with my wife, there's a lesson to be learned by me.

Here's another thing about my wife: She is always right. It's not that she always has to be right (and I have to be wrong); it's just that she is. It irks me a bit, but I don't begrudge her for that. In fact, in an odd way, I admire her for it; hell, I would settle for being right one out of ten times.

You must understand that a lot of husbands just aren't right very often in the eyes of their wives (this doesn't happen right away, perhaps after two or three years of marriage) and most guys eventually just accept it. This isn't just my opinion—ask just about any guy who has been married for, let's say, three or more years, and you'll see what I mean.

In the film *The Blind Side,* there's a scene when Tim McGraw's character Sean tells Sandra Bullock's character Leigh Anne what he believes is the gift of Michael Oher, the homeless teen they took in. After listening to him, Leigh Anne begrudgingly says to Sean, "You're right." Upon hearing those two words from his wife, his eyes light up as if he just scored a rare victory. He is so pleasantly shocked to hear "You're right" come out of her mouth that he asks her how the words taste, and she says, "Like vinegar." Here's one more example of how wrong we husbands usually are: Mike Greenberg, the long-time co-host of ESPN Radio's *Mike and Mike in the Morning* wrote a book several years ago titled, *Why My Wife Thinks I'm an Idiot.* An apropos book title if there ever was one.

You've probably heard the expression, "pick your battles." Nowhere is "pick your battles" more applicable than when arguing (or potentially arguing) with your wife. In years one through five of our marriage, when an argument with my wife was imminent, I would pick a battle—that is, argue with her—about 50 percent of the time. In years five through ten, it dropped to about 20 percent. From year ten on, it dropped to single digits—low single digits—and keeps dropping. Today, it's about 0.5 percent of the time.

Okay, so how can you crack your wife's code and avoid a TKO when you argue with her? Like a boxer preparing for a prizefight, study your opponent. Following is a selective sampling of words and phrases, along with the true hidden meaning women carefully choose to use when they are arguing. While you are probably familiar with the established definitions that are found in *Webster's Dictionary,* within the secret language of women, these words and phrases take on whole new meanings.

Fine

When your wife is mad at you, *nothing* is fine. In fact, it's the opposite of fine. *Fine* means "It's *not* fine." During an argument, your wife will say "fine" when she's proven she is right and wants to shut you up. This is a bad sign.

Nothing

Nothing definitely means something, and you should be on high alert. When your wife says *nothing,* as in "Nothing is wrong," you can be sure that something *is* definitely wrong—and you are probably the culprit behind that nothing.

Go ahead (with arched eyebrows)

This is a dare, and your wife is testing you. You will hear "Go ahead" from her when you say you are going to do something that will push her pissed-off level off the charts. She's saying "go ahead" to you, but her eyebrows are saying, "He can't possibly be *that* foolish."

Exaggerated sigh

A sigh may not be a verbal statement, but it carries *a lot* of meaning. Basically, it means your wife thinks you are being completely juvenile at the moment and is wondering, *Why am I with this man?*

That's okay

No, it is *not* okay. When your wife is mad at you, this is one of the most deceptive things she will say to you. "That's okay" is her way of internalizing what's happened and how she feels about it; women tend to do this much more deeply than us guys. So when your wife says, "That's okay," she is really wondering how on earth you couldn't possibly know that it is *not* okay.

Please do

This is a generous offer from your wife, giving you the opportunity to explain why you have done something that, to her, is inexcusable. This offer doesn't come along often, so think long and hard about what you are going to say, but don't wait too long and blow your chance.

Thanks a lot

No, she is not thanking you. Delivered with stinging sarcasm, "Thanks a lot," means your wife appreciates what you said or did (or both) about as much as Michelle Obama appreciates Donald Trump.

That's interesting

You will hear this in response to something you have said or done that your wife has no interest in whatsoever. Or, in some cases, this might actually mean, "Are you kidding me?! You can't be serious!" In the first instance, she might say, "That's interesting" when you begin to tell her about where you stand in your fantasy football league. In the second case, the "that's interesting" will be laced with something more bitter—for example, if you suggest spending your anniversary or Valentine's Day at a sporting event or watching *Animal House*.

You exhaust me*

This phrase has no hidden meaning: you are literally exhausting your wife. You will likely hear this phrase

---

*This is one that I heard quite often early on in our marriage. My brother Chris's wife says it, too. Take it literally if this phrase ever passes your wife's lips.

when you have said or done something that, to her, is so dimwitted and idiotic that you have pushed her to the edge and she no longer has the energy to argue with you. She is drained. She has given up and will probably walk away in sheer disgust. This, however, doesn't mean you've won the argument—think of it like half-time and your wife will come out with a vengeance to begin the second half.

Look, even though I have shared the meaning of various phrases your wife may use when arguing with you, I'm going to reiterate what I told you before: avoid arguing with her at all costs. Even if you hear some of the aforementioned phrases and have a better understanding of where she is coming from, your response probably won't change the situation to your advantage. I asked five married friends—guys who have been married for at least ten years—if they feel they ever win an argument with their wives. After they stopped laughing, their answers ranged from "Are you kidding me?" to "No effing way!" to "That's a stupid question."

My wife and I rarely argue these days. First off, we're older, wiser, and more mature (well, at least one of us is). Also, what's the point of arguing when I know I'm going to lose?

6

Social Events:
Study the Game Plan

"A man in love is incomplete until he
is married. Then he's finished."

—ZSA ZSA GABOR

You're going to face many new and unexpected challenges as a married man. You're going to have to be more fiscally responsible. You're going to have to be more community-oriented. You're going to have to become more mature (or at least fake it), and you're going to have to be an exemplary father, son-in-law, and perhaps brother-in-law.

While marriage has many daunting challenges, perhaps one of the biggest challenges you will ever face (especially early on in your marriage) is getting through an entire social occasion—be it a wedding reception, birthday party, or even a dinner party with friends—from start to finish without saying or doing something that will embarrass your wife. Believe me, it's going to happen (probably several times), so there's no use denying it.

I've been there, and every one of my married friends

has been there as well. And here's the kicker: At the time you commit a social faux pas that will make the veins in your wife's neck stick out, you and your buddies who are present at the time won't even know that you did something wrong. Unless your wife immediately intervenes (which she likely won't do to spare herself the embarrassment), you'll keep saying or doing whatever it is that has set her off, blissfully ignorant of the fuse you just lit.

As you know, when you're single and you get together with your guy friends to watch a football game, the gathering is one dimensional and there is one agenda: watch the game, drink some beers, eat some pizza and/or wings, and between quarters and half-time, check your fantasy football team's points and talk about, among other things, the latest action movies, how much work sucks, and the latest idiotic postings on Facebook. It's a simple and innocuous gathering. When you're with your buddies, every time you open your mouth you could (and you probably do) say something offensive, and the great part is they really don't care as long as there is cold beer and food readily available. We men can be quite simple creatures.

Our wives, on the other hand, play by a completely different set of rules during social gatherings, and it's usually during the drive home (which I'll address later) that your wife will tell you with laser-like accuracy exactly what you did wrong, why it was wrong, and how you embarrassed her yet again.

With married women, social occasions, especially get-togethers that involve several other women, are multidimensional, and there are multiple agendas layered with implication and hidden innuendo. There will be shit going on right in front of you that immediately registers with every woman present, and you and your buddies will be absolutely clueless about what is happening. It's almost like you're not even at the same function. You'll really have no idea what you're getting yourself into, and before you know it, you'll be swimming with the social sharks.

When a group of married couples gets together, it's like some of the women in the group are competing for the Good Housekeeping Seal of Approval for Social Etiquette. And unbeknownst to every guy in the group, their wives have entered them into the competition, and every move they make and every word that comes out of their respective mouths is being closely scrutinized by the judges (the women present).

Once you get married, you are playing in an entirely new and advanced social league. It's like you've been called up to Major League Baseball during the World Series after playing only one game in Triple A ball. You're in way over your head.

Going to a social event with your wife can be like being a professional athlete prepping for a playoff game. Some wives view social events much like a coach views prepping his team for a playoff game. The coach (your wife) will spend hours studying film of the other team (the people you will be interacting and bullshitting with), and she will prepare a game plan that she will review with you while you are getting dressed for the event and/or driving there.

For me, virtually all of this "coaching" occurred early on in my marriage. On our way to a function, Lissette would say things like, "You know that we can't talk about Steve and Lisa dating in front of Diane" (I didn't know), or "I don't want you telling Jane that Cindy and I are getting together tomorrow for breakfast" (Why the hell would I?), or "Under no circumstances are you to ask Karen and Brad if they are still trying to have a baby" (I thought they already did).

After my wife drilled the game plan into my head, she would say something like, "You know, I shouldn't have to tell you these things." (So, why are you?) I strongly believe this "game plan" thing is a function of women having wider social circles than men and also that women tend to compartmentalize social interactions. Men rarely do this.

Just like a football or baseball game, once you arrive at your destination, you are on the field of play with the other players, and the coach, while usually within earshot, can't control your every action on the field. That's when you are most vulnerable to committing an error or penalty.

Several years ago, close friends of ours had a brunch reception at a local restaurant after they baptized their son. When we arrived at the restaurant, we went to the private room where the brunch was being held. I went up to the bar and ordered two beers, one for a friend and one for me. The bartender asked if I wanted some glasses and I said no.

Unbeknownst to me at the time, this was Penalty #1. After my friend and I finished our beers, I headed back to the bar, and just as I was about to order another round, my wife intercepted me, telling me that "We're not at a fraternity party" and that I should drink my beer from a glass.

In the private room where the reception was being held were five round tables set up for guests: four tables were placed around the perimeter of the room and one was in the middle. As we were about to sit down, my wife asked me where I would like to sit. I looked at the center table where my nephew (who was ten years old at the time) was already sitting and said, "Why don't we sit there with Michael" and I started making my way toward the table.

This was Penalty #2. Based on my decision, my brother, his wife, my nephew, my niece, my wife, and I would have occupied six of the eight chairs at the center table, which (to my surprise) was apparently designated the "head" table for the hosts of the gathering. I felt my wife tug on my arm as she led me away from the center table toward one of the four perimeter tables. It was a perfect audible; it was as if she went up to the line of scrimmage, saw the defense, and changed the play on the move. At the time I didn't know why she changed the play. Of course, I quickly learned why on the drive home.

Lissette is cognizant of proper etiquette and behavior in social settings. Unlike me, she always knows the right thing to say and do when we're at a social event—it's like she's had private lessons with Emily Post. It's a very admirable quality, one that I will likely never possess.

Furthermore, my wife's brain works like a PC's

central processing unit. We could be at a party or event for five hours, and when I inevitably say or do something wrong, even if we've only been there for ten minutes, she immediately and automatically stores it in her mind and continues to do so for every other faux pas I commit during the gathering.

On the drive home, she calls up the files she saved and unloads, telling me with pinpoint accuracy exactly what I did wrong, why it was wrong, and how I embarrassed her. It really is quite amazing how she records and processes this information—it's like she has a hidden camera following me around capturing my every word and action.

My wife has super hearing power like the bionic woman, and I bet your wife does, too. She could be in deep conversation with a friend on the other side of the room and somehow she'll hear something I said that, according to her, "wasn't appropriate" for such a function.

At our friend's son's baptism, we weren't even out of the restaurant parking lot when she pulled up the footage from her hidden camera and told me about the center table averted faux pas, as well as three or four other things I did wrong at the brunch.

While the drive home is usually treated like a post-game breakdown of the game plan gone bad, when (it's not a matter of *if*) you commit a social faux pas your wife may not wait until the drive home and will attempt to remedy the situation during the game action.

There are two tried-and-true ways that your wife will attempt to do this. The first is to give you *The*

Look. If you haven't already experienced it, *The Look* is a piercing, unrelenting, and merciless stare. If women had super powers (which some do), *The Look* would allow them to shoot a laser beam from their eyes that would not only make you shut up, it would pierce the front and back of your skull.

With *The Look,* your wife is attempting to communicate with you in a nonverbal fashion. Although she may look calm and reserved on the outside, on the inside she is screaming, "Shut up right now before you embarrass me even more than you already have!" If your wife gives you a look and it registers with you, whatever you do, *don't* look at her and say, "What did I do?" I've done that, and believe me, asking that question is worse than not noticing *The Look.*

The second tried-and-true way your wife will attempt to redirect or quell your well-intended but misguided comments is a more direct, physical way: *The Kick* or *The Thigh Squeeze.* Unlike *The Look,* which she can unleash on you any time during a social get-together, your wife will only resort to *The Kick* or *Thigh Squeeze* if you're both sitting down and you're within striking distance under the convenient protection of a tablecloth.

Let's say you're having dinner with friends and you say something that only the women in the room find offensive. If you're seated next to your wife, she will kick you in the shin or reach over and squeeze your thigh. As with *The Look,* if she does one or the other, do not ask her, "Why are you kicking (or squeezing) me?" I've asked that of my wife once or twice (you'd think I would have learned after the first time), and it has made many bad situations even worse.

Look, I've been married for more than two decades, and I occasionally still embarrass my wife at social functions with something I've said or done. Don't sweat it if, like me, it takes you years to improve (in the eyes of your wife) your social etiquette. As Lissette once said to me, "Even after all these years of marriage, I can't believe there are still times when I have to babysit you when we're around other people."

7.

Home Life:
It's Her Domain

"Women! Can't live with them
. . . pass the beer nuts."

—NORM FROM THE NBC COMEDY *CHEERS*

In 1999 my wife and I moved into our current home, which is a 1928 Spanish-style house in a neighborhood that we long desired to live in. We loved the house from the moment we saw it, and when we bought it, we knew we would be in it for decades to come.

Shortly after we moved in, my close friend Jim, who I grew up with in Rhode Island, came to visit my brothers and me in Southern California. When Jim and I arrived at my home from the airport, my wife wasn't there, so I gave him the grand tour. We walked through the living room, dining room, kitchen, and family room downstairs. I then took him upstairs and showed him the master and guest bedrooms, bathrooms, and balcony off the master bedroom overlooking our courtyard. I also pointed out the artwork and paintings on the walls.

As we were walking downstairs, I heard Jim laughing to himself, so I turned around and he had an ear-to-ear grin on his face and was shaking his head. "What are you laughing about?" I asked.

While still laughing, he said, "It is so clear that after spending just five minutes here that you have absolutely no influence whatsoever over the decoration of this house."

Jim was single at the time.

When you move into a house, condominium, or apartment with your wife, be prepared to not only relinquish whatever limited sense of style you possess but to also acquiesce your sovereign right to land. You may have just purchased a three-bedroom, three-bathroom house, but in reality, if you're lucky, you'll get one wall of one room that you can call your own. Case in point: I have more than fifteen framed photos and magazine covers and seven pennants touting the Patriots' five Super Bowl victories and the Red Sox 2004, 2007, and 2013 World Series titles. Every one of these items is proudly displayed in one place in my house: the garage.

While your and your wife's names may be on the mortgage documents or rental agreement, you are now in her domain. Your house is her sphere of influence. The well-known adage, "This place needs a woman's touch," must have originated from a married man who was trying to get back at his single guy friends.

My wife and I are Catholic, and we did not live together until we were married—it was more her choice than mine, but that's another story. Thus, like virtually everything that is inherent with marriage, I had no idea what I was in for and had to make some fairly big adjustments.

Buying your first home with your wife is an emotional roller-coaster ride. You're teaming with anticipation and saying to yourself, "I'm finally a homeowner and I can't wait to move in." It's your abode and you're the king of the castle, right? You'll picture in your mind a man cave featuring a new 65-inch curved LCD TV, your sports memorabilia, and maybe a built-in barbecue in the backyard. Then comes moving day, and that's when your fantasy abruptly ends because she takes over. For good.

For generations, millions of married men from all walks of life have tried to figure out why this happens; it's like there's an explicit contract signed by both parties during the engagement period that states, "Upon moving into our first home together, and every home thereafter, I (fill in your name here) will abdicate all decisions concerning household furnishings, decorations, artwork, and general aesthetics to my wife-to-be." Sign on the dotted line. It's an unseen ironclad contract that is as enforceable as any prenuptial agreement. On moving day, my wife took over our home with the deft precision of a special operations military exercise.

When you and your wife purchase your first home, you are going to see things in your house that will make you and your friends' heads spin. Women mark their territory much like a cat, and the marking of territory can actually start outside the house at the front door.

When we bought our house, the ordinary "Welcome" mat was replaced by a mat with three little monkeys in the "Hear No Evil, Speak No Evil, and See No Evil" poses. The monkeys are dressed in little vests and hats. Cute, right?

Inside your home you could see things similar to the items that my wife has decorated our home with such as antique irons, a small statue of the Virgin Mary, wall sconces shaped like angels, and bowls of potpourri that have such scents as Apple Cinnamon and Pine Forest.

Your wife will also place more candles in rooms throughout your house than Jimmy Carter has on his birthday cake. My wife has a carved wooden horse that sits in the foyer at the top of the stairs just outside our bedroom; I can't tell you how many times I've stubbed my big toe on the hoof of that damn horse. The horse, which measures four feet by two-and-a-half feet, should be on the merry-go-round at an amusement park, but it's not. It's in our hallway, and I don't quite understand why.

A close friend and his wife bought their first house about a year after they were married. About a month after they moved in, I visited him, and sitting there on his kitchen counter was a small bronze statue of a ballerina. Every time my friend, who's six-foot-two and weighs about 210 pounds, goes to pour himself a cup of coffee in the morning, he has to look at that diminutive dancer on her tiptoes staring back at him. "I really would like to shove her and her tutu down the garbage disposal," he said to me. Of course, he knows that statue is there for good.

In your master bedroom, your bed will have a duvet (it's basically a bed spread), and for some reason, the customary two pillows just won't do anymore. Your wife could have six to eight pillows of various sizes and colors on your bed, and here's the kicker: when you guys go to sleep at night, you'll still use only your pillow and she will use only her pillow.

For reasons unexplained, wives find it necessary to cover nearly half of the bed with these superfluous pillows during the day. I mean they just sit there taking up space and gathering dust. It's a real pain because at night when you're tired and all you want to do is go to sleep, you have to take the extra pillows off the bed, and in the morning, you have to put them back on the bed. It's a never-ending cycle.

If your wife is as passionate about her culture as my wife is about hers, you will see items in your house that you thought you would only find in a history museum or art gallery. Lissette cherishes any item that embodies her Hispanic culture and can't be found at Pottery Barn. For example, she adores the pair of oversized wooden carvings of heads that now sit atop our grandfather clock. I'm told that these *Gigantes* (translated: Giants)—one is a man's head and one is a woman's head—are used for ceremonial-type festivals and celebrations in Guatemala. Anyway, the first time I saw these giant heads was shortly after Lissette had placed them on top of the armoire in our bedroom. They were literally staring down at our bed. One day after work while I was changing my clothes, I looked up and suddenly there they were, mocking me in my underwear.

They freaked me out. And here's another example: Upon returning home from a trip to visit friends in Guatemala, my wife showed me a painting that she bought during her visit.

I looked at it and asked her, "Who's the sheep and the kid?"

"Honey," she said, "it's the Lamb of God with baby Jesus."

Today, the sheep and the kid painting is prominently displayed in our living room along with the two *Gigantes*. (There was no way in hell I was going to bed every night with those giant heads staring down at me.)

In addition to artwork and other aesthetic household items, your wife will choose your household furnishing, and when it comes to your furniture, be prepared to move it around a few times a year at your wife's behest. We weren't in our house for more than ten months before my wife had me moving around the sofas, chairs, and tables in our living room, which by far is the largest room in our house and has the most furniture. Even though the room looked fine to me, Lissette just wasn't content with keeping the living room furniture in its original place. As I was straining my lower back while moving a chair, she told me that the way we originally set up the living room furniture just didn't satisfy her sense of aesthetics.

Now that you have a clear picture of what happens when you and your wife buy a house, you also need to be prepared for one other domestic ritual from her that is a tradition as old as marriage itself: the dreaded to-do (or honey-do) list. When Neanderthal men roamed the earth, I imagine their to-do lists included such chores as sweeping out the cave and killing a Woolly Mammoth or two for dinner. Since that period, like man, to-do lists have evolved, and as a husband, your to-do list will regularly include such chores as cleaning the garage, cutting the lawn, washing dishes, cooking, and the ever-popular taking out the trash.

I've heard from friends whose wives post their to-do lists in highly visible areas such as taped to a six-pack of beer in the refrigerator. Some wives have their husband's weekend planned out for them and measure their success based on how many items they can scratch off the respective to-do lists by Sunday night.

When you move into your first place together, I recommend the method that was used during the Great Land Rush of the late 1800s. On moving day, treat it like a land grab and run into the house before your wife and declare ownership of a room (other than the living room, dining room, kitchen, den, and master bedroom, all of which she will claim under eminent domain).

Start big and if she acquiesces, great. If your wife gives you the standard, "I don't think so," then at least negotiate down from there. You may end up with at least one wall in one room that you can call your own. This worked for me (sort of) as I staked unequivocal claim to a "room"—my garage. A garage has spiders, and as a general rule, most women hate spiders. Most married women I know spend little time in their respective garages.

If your father is anything like my dad, you know that the garage is, indeed, a place where you look forward to spending time. When we were kids, my brothers and I would spend hours in the garage with our dad. A garage, perhaps even more so than your den that houses your large-screen TV, is the ideal place for male bonding.

I have a friend who has a five-bedroom house that's about three thousand square feet. When we get together to play poker at his house, we play in one place: his garage. My father-in-law loves drinking beer and watching golf or soccer in his garage for hours on end. Hell, he'd probably sleep every night in his garage if he could get away with it.

In your garage, along with your tools, rolls of duct tape, and WD-40, you can put up your pennants, posters, and other guy stuff. You can retreat there to appreciate the simple pleasures of Craftsman tools and an aging workbench along with a mini refrigerator filled with beer. I live in Southern California and because of occasional earthquakes, the majority of homes here don't have basements. If you live in any of the other forty-nine states, just about everything I said about a garage carries over to your basement. Make one (or both if you have them) of those rooms yours.

8.

Closets and Bathrooms: She Came, She Saw, She Conquered

"I think men who have a pierced ear are better prepared for marriage. They have experienced pain and bought jewelry."

—RITA RUDNER

Nowhere does the "It's Her Domain" principle apply more than in your—or what you thought were your—bathrooms and closets. Wives commandeer closets and bathrooms with the swiftness and force of a Navy Seals unit. You will be shocked and awed once you see how quickly your wife seizes control of these spaces in your home.

I'm not saying that you necessarily *want* to have control of these rooms. I'm just saying that you will feel like a stranger in a foreign land the first time you sit on the throne after your wife does her extreme bathroom makeover. To steal a phrase from the erstwhile conqueror Julius Caesar, when it came to the bathrooms and closets in our new home, *veni vidi vici*—or rather, *venit vidisset vinceret:* she came, she saw, she conquered.

If you buy an older house like ours with limited closet space, be prepared to put your clothes in any closet except the master bedroom closet. On the day we moved into our first home, I mistakenly tried to put my clothes in our closet. Lissette walked into our bedroom behind me and with a puzzled look on her face asked, "What are you doing?" When I told her that I was putting my clothes in what I thought was our closet, she quickly corrected me and pointed me in the direction of the guest bedroom. "Honey, you'll be keeping your clothes in the closet in the other room," she said. We weren't even in the house for a day, and my wife immediately assumed de facto closet squatting rights.

Occasionally, such as when my wife goes shopping for new clothes, her closets overflow and she puts some of her clothes in my closet. I don't dare encroach on her closet space. In fact, in more than twenty years of marriage, I have never—and I mean never—put one of my shirts or pair of pants in the closet in our master bedroom; it's our bedroom, but it's her closet.

On the contrary, in addition to putting her overflow in my closet, Lissette has designated my closet as a makeshift mini-storage where she keeps gifts. I'm not talking about gifts she buys for a birthday party or wedding that we have to go to in a week or two. I'm talking about gifts she purchases "to have just in case." For example, during a recent check of gifts in my closet, among other things, I found:

- 12 decorative picture frames
- 8 pairs of chopsticks my wife purchased in Japan
- 6 scented candles
- 5 children's DVDs
- 1 Matchbox 5-Pack Car Set (which I think I'll keep)
- 3 Sesame Street Take Along Grover dolls
- 1 Barbie doll
- 1 "Sing and Giggle" Winnie The Pooh
- 1 Spiderman lunchbox

I have more gifts for other people in my closet than I have clothes for myself. Some of the gifts—hell, most of them—have been there for years, overflowing from the chest of drawers in my closet onto the floor. I'll admit at first this encroachment on my closet irked me; however, I got used to it years ago, and it's now normal to see new gifts there from time to time.

The bathroom is another opportunity for your wife to stockpile seemingly countless items that take up more space than the toilet, tub, and sink combined. I read an article online that said the average number of items in a typical woman's bathroom is 337. For men, the average number is 6. That's mind boggling if you think about it.

Not only will your wife hoard innumerable traditional bathroom products for herself, if she's like my wife, she may be inclined to experiment a bit. For example, there were once rocks in the sink in our guest bathroom downstairs. I kid you not; I counted thirty-nine small stones in the sink (you know, the shiny kind you may have collected as a kid).

One day I went in there to wash my hands, and there they were. I had no idea why they were in the sink until my wife told me that some woman who is a so-called Feng Shui expert told her to put them there because they provide "positive energy" in the room. Why we needed positive energy in the bathroom is a mystery to me. It's only fitting that of all the rooms in our house, the rocks were in a bathroom because in my opinion the whole Feng Shui thing is a crock of you know what. Do you want to know what *Feng Shui* really means? It means throw your husband's shit in the garage.

The shower is another place your wife takes nothing for granted and leaves nothing to chance. Have you ever seen how many products a typical wife has in her shower? It can reach double digits. In this way, wives are like Boy Scouts—they are always prepared. As a guy, you know that all you need in your shower is a bar of soap and shampoo (or a two-in-one bodywash/shampoo). That's it. Why on earth would you need anything else? Get in, soap down, wash your hair (if you're north of fifty like I am, what you have left of it), rinse, and then dry off. Bing, bang, boom—you're done in about five to seven minutes.

On the other end of the spectrum, we have our wives who have more than just soap and shampoo—much more than that—in the shower. In our shower, my bottle of 2-in-1 bodywash/shampoo is typically outnumbered by about ten to one. Not only does Lissette have her everyday shampoo, soap, and conditioner, but she also has her "special" (read: *overpriced*) shampoos, conditioners, soaps, gels, oils, and bodywash, which are strictly off limits to me (not that I'd want to use the stuff anyway).

During her shower, Lissette sticks with a routine that would make the contestants on *America's Next Top Model* proud. She applies her "Visibly Even" foaming cleanser (which promises "more even toned, radiant skin") to her facecloth and washes her face. Then she applies another product on another cloth (this one is not a facecloth because it's used for the rest of her body). She also has a pair of little purple gloves (I'm not kidding) that she uses to exfoliate. I'm not sure why she uses the little gloves, and to be honest, I've never been compelled to ask her about them. I just don't care to know. In addition to her foaming cleanser, while showering Lissette typically uses:

o Body lotion

o A "Leave-in Treatment" (I think this is shampoo)

o Conditioning balm

o Shower gel/*moussant*

o Skin Brightening Daily Scrub

o Body oil for "a sheer moisturizing experience"

You get the picture. I would love for Lissette to go for one month without using any of her special shower items. She could use my 2-in-1 bodywash/shampoo, and I am certain she would look just as good as she always does.

Before I started using the combo bodywash/shampoo, I had no choice but to use another bar of soap I found in our bathroom cabinet when I ran out of my bar of Irish Spring. Little did I know that what I chose to use was a subcategory of my wife's special soap: guest soap. At that time, I did not know that our guests required different soap than us, which like my wife's special shampoo is off limits to me. However, within a day or two, Lissette saw that I had been using the guest soap in the shower and made it clear to me that the guest soap (hence the name) is not for me and to not use it.

While the special guest soap is off limits to me, my guy friends, being that they are our guests, are allowed to use it when they are at our house. In fact, when a friend was once visiting us, he gave me a hard time about the flowery-scented soap he had to use in the bathroom. I told him that my wife put the special soap out for guests and to get over it. He then told me that his wife does the same thing and that he isn't allowed to use the guest soap in his bathroom.

So the twisted irony with the special guest soap rule is that there's special soap in my house that I am not allowed to use that my friends are allowed to use, and there's special soap in my friends' homes that they aren't allowed to use that I am allowed to use. I'd love for someone to explain that logic to me someday.

Two bars of soap are stored in our bathroom

cabinet that are respectively labeled "Dewberry," which is purplish, and "Juniper," which is green. Dewberry and Juniper are not only designated as guest soap by my wife but also the wrappers state that the soaps are "for use by adults only." Juniper and Dewberry are the first bars of soap I have ever seen that are rated and discriminate against kids. Aside from the scents, I have no idea how they are different from regular soap and why they are not to be used by kids.

In addition to the customary shower staples of soap and shampoo that have served you just fine all these years, you will discover that your wife will have countless other items that take up space in your shower and in the bathroom. On a random check of our bathroom cabinets, right next to my wife's "weightless conditioner" and "cucumber melon body splash," I found a bottle of "Lavender Bath, Body & Linen Water." I have no idea what linen water is—I didn't even know that it exists; it does, and Lissette sprays it on herself just about every time after she showers. Lissette's bottle of linen water isn't small—it's 32 ounces with a trigger on top. I practically trip over the damn thing every time I push back our leopard skin–patterned shower curtain to get in the shower.

There's one other upside to my wife's bottle of linen water—it's multifunctional. The instructions (yes, instructions) on the bottle state that in addition to spraying on the body, the linen water can be used on "linens, bedding, fabric, furniture, or in any room as an air freshener." It's by far the most multifunctional toiletry item I've ever seen.

I don't know one guy who loses sleep over the fact that his wife has taken over their bathrooms and closets. I got used to it several years ago. Like many things that "come with the territory" of marriage, just accept it and go with the flow.

9.

The Other Woman

"I was married by a judge.
I should have asked for a jury."

—GROUCHO MARX

I am going to give you some of the most unorthodox advice you will ever receive from a married man. Now, before I go on, what you are about to read will at first seem so ludicrous and so farfetched that you may ask yourself, *What the hell is this guy smoking?* You may even be inclined to immediately dismiss everything I have already shared with you and toss this book in the trash. But trust me, I speak from experience and would not lead you down the wrong path.

In fact, I believe the very unconventional guidance you are about to receive is, in many ways, the equivalent of receiving investing advice from Warren Buffett (okay, that probably is a bit of a stretch). Put another way, I'm going to let you in on a key ingredient of the secret sauce of marital bliss, after about three or four years of marriage.

Here's my advice: if your wife has a sister (or any variation of a close female) she gets along with who is ever in need of a place to stay on a temporary basis, invite her to stay at your house. If you have the extra room, don't hesitate to say, "*Mi casa es su casa.*"

Stupid idea? Why on earth would I give you such seemingly misguided advice? Keep reading.

Before my wife and I had kids, we had, at separate times, two female houseguests. My wife's sister, Donna, stayed with us for about one year shortly after we bought our first house, and then at a later time, my wife's cousin, Michelle, stayed with us for the better part of one year.

Why would any married man want to live with two women? I'll tell you why: because when we had The Other Woman living in our house, not once did Lissette ask me questions like "When is this game going to be over?" or "Are you going to spend your entire day watching football?" or "Do you have to watch SportsCenter every night?"

Do you see where I'm going here? Are you beginning to understand why you should follow my lead on this?

Having The Other Woman in your house is your free hall pass to watch as much sports on TV as you possibly can, binge watch your favorite Netflix series, and take in your favorite guy movies—the ones you watched and made fun of when you were single and living with your buddies. Do you think you can possibly obtain that type of unrestricted freedom when it's just you and your wife? Hell no.

When The Other Woman is around, your wife and she will slide into their dimension while you slide into your dimension. They are simpatico, so not only does having The Other Woman in your house make it possible for you to do your thing, it can also get you out of doing some of the things you probably don't look forward to, such as going shopping with your wife or watching a chick flick with her. You can retire to your own corner of the house and, if you are a sports fan, depending on the season, watch hour after hour of football, baseball, or basketball. As long as the ladies are doing their own thing, your wife won't lay a guilt trip on you. The Other Woman is a 24/7 built-in buffer that mitigates many of the sacrifices you normally have to make as a married man.

There were several times when all three of us— Lissette, Donna/Michelle, and I—were home, but it was like we lived in separate houses. On Sundays during football season, when my wife and The Other Woman went shopping, out to eat, or even if they just retired to the backyard, I watched nearly every game on DIRECTV's NFL Sunday Ticket package, the Sunday night game, and after that, highlights on ESPN. Of course, watching Monday Night Football was never a problem as long as The Other Woman was in our house.

Here's another plus: if your buddies text you one night and tell you to meet them for a few beers at a local bar, it's never a problem when The Other Woman is around. And, believe it or not, your wife might actually (temporarily) take on some of your former guy roommates' character traits and let things slide while The Other Woman is around. It's like she has been hypnotized to give you more slack than ever before. However, I have to underscore that such a metamorphosis is temporary. Once The Other Woman moves out, your wife will snap out of this state as quickly as a Clayton Kershaw fastball reaches home plate.

Here's a true story, and it is one of the best examples I can think of that illustrates the value of The Other Woman. Years ago, on a typical Friday afternoon, when we did not have The Other Woman staying with us, I was sitting in my office and a good friend called to say that he was putting together an impromptu poker game that night at his house. He said he'd spoken with my brothers and a few other friends and they were all in.

I told him I was pretty certain I could play because, as far as I knew, Lissette and I didn't have anything planned. I told him I just needed to call Lissette to let her know I'd be home late.

When I called my wife, she reminded me of a previous commitment. "Honey," she said, "don't you remember? We have a reception at a neighbor's house to meet the new director of the local opera."

I slumped in my chair and felt as if I had been sucker punched in the gut. "Oh," I said, "somehow it must have slipped my mind."

As you have probably gathered by now, I am not an opera-type of guy. Well, with my tail tucked between my legs, I called my friend back and told him about the opera director meet-and-greet reception. Of course, while I had him on the phone, he got my brother Chris on the line and the two of them told me what a wimp I was, and basically beat the proverbial shit out of me.

They even offered to call Lissette to remind her that I'd likely say or do something that would embarrass her at such a highbrow and hoity-toity reception. (If memory serves me correctly, I did say something at the reception that embarrassed her.)

The point I am making with this sad little anecdote is that if Donna or Michelle had been living with us at the time, my wife would have gladly gone to the reception with The Other Woman, and I would have been able to spend that Friday evening drinking beer and playing high/low and Texas hold 'em with the boys instead of learning the history of cantata, cavatina, and castrato.

I may have given you the impression that I don't like spending time with my wife. I want to be clear that nothing could be further from the truth. Along with my daughters, there's no one else I would rather spend my time with. I very much enjoy being with her, and we do have several common interests that connect us beyond husband and wife. All I'm saying is that I don't think it's healthy for any two people to spend every waking minute together, and I believe that having The Other Woman temporarily in your house—after you've been married for a handful of years—will allow you to enjoy your leisurely pursuits without feeling guilty and your wife can bond with her girlfriend at the same time.

Also, all kidding aside, you will be helping out someone in need who is close to your wife—it's a win-win-win situation.

10.

You're a Real Romantic

"Marriage is an adventure, like going to war."

—G. K. CHESTERTON

I'm pretty sure you already know that the woman in your life likely prefers romance movies to just about any other film genre. If she doesn't, she's an exception. Women love to break out a box of Kleenex tissue and become engrossed in the formulaic, syrupy chick flicks that Hollywood churns out. And, of course, more often than not, they want us to sit through the excruciatingly long movie with them.

Look, I know I'm not letting you in on a big secret. Telling you that your wife likes romance movies is like telling you Steph Curry is a pretty good three-point shooter. I know I'm stating the obvious. However, for those of you who are uninitiated, I am going to let you in on a little known—albeit extremely important—consequence of watching a romance movie with your wife. But before I let you in on that little secret, be sure to take this advice to heart: if you can, after you've been married awhile, avoid watching romance movies with your wife—and not just because you have little interest in the film. I know this is a big stretch, but do it anyway. It doesn't matter if the movie is on the big screen, small screen, or iPad—somehow, someway find a valid (or invalid) reason to *not* watch that movie with your wife.

Okay, now allow me to explain why: A few years into our marriage, my wife rented (this was when Blockbuster was still around) a romance movie called *Bed of Roses,* and she asked me to watch it with her.

Bed of Roses stars Christian Slater as a widower who quit his job as a New York stockbroker and opened his own flower shop. (Right then and there, I knew I was in for a long night.) While I won't bore you with the minutia, Slater's character found the new love of his life, and in a few scenes, he sneaked into her apartment and decorated it with an assortment of flowers. While we were watching the movie, every now and then—in between looking at my watch hoping I wouldn't miss SportsCenter (this was before DVRs so I couldn't record it)—I would glance over at my wife and she would be wiping away tears. Lissette's box of tissue was right by her side.

At the end of the movie, as the credits were rolling and just as I geared up to watch ESPN, without warning, my wife looked at me with weepy eyes and said, "You never do anything romantic like that anymore. Why can't you be more romantic like Christian Slater's character?"

I was cornered. I was all set to catch the day's sports highlights, and she threw me a curveball when I wasn't even expecting a pitch.

So therein lies the problem with watching a romance movie with your wife after you have been married for a few years. At the end of the movie, while the story is still fresh on her mind and she is emotionally spent, there is a very good chance she will compare what she saw on screen with her life, the life she chose to spend with you. Of course, there's just no comparison between you and Hollywood's depiction of Mr. Romance. Hollywood makes all of us married guys look like romance school dropouts.

After watching the movie, my wife not only accused me of being an unromantic clod, she challenged me to tell her how many times I had done something romantic for her in the prior two or three months. "You can't think of any, can you?" This challenge caught me off guard. But it won't catch you off guard: Be prepared when your wife does the very same thing, which is very much in the realm of possibility.

Nowhere does the expression "suspend disbelief" apply more than to romance films. While watching a romance film, wives conveniently forget that they are viewing complete fiction. Joseph Gordon-Levitt's character Jon in the 2013 movie *Don Jon* perfectly summed up the opposite viewpoint of romance films between men and women when he said to his friend, "Everyone knows it's fake but they watch it like it's real life." On the contrary, on CNN's original series, *The History of Comedy,* the actress Rachel Bloom gave a woman's point of view on romance films. She said, "We have a love-hate relationship with romantic films because it sets these ideals that you can never reach, but love is so relatable you immediately empathize with one of the people and you feel like you're falling in love." Do you think you will ever hear a guy say something like that?

Additionally, the irony with romance movies is that the dashing leading man who sweeps the actress off her feet often turns out to be a douchebag in real life. (I will prove this point before the end of this chapter.) But most wives don't buy that at the time. They have seen what they believe is a new romance benchmark and that there are guys out there who actually do this kind of stuff on a regular basis.

As a guy, you know that early on in a relationship, you will make the extra effort to wine and dine your girlfriend—it's a natural part of an evolving relationship. During a monologue for his show, Seth Meyers, the comedian and host of *Late Night with Seth Meyers*, talked about how guys are markedly different while "courting" a woman. He said, "While courting, you do things to impress her like going apple picking and taking those apples home and making a pie. Once you actually become a couple, you're not going apple picking and making pies anymore."

After maybe three or four years as husband and wife, your romance routine wanes, and it runs the risk of slipping into a semi-moribund state with every passing year. It's not like you become less romantic on purpose. But once kids come along—coupled with the daily hectic life most of us lead—it just happens naturally over time, like a thinning hairline and expanding waistline.

I will admit that when my wife put me on the spot after watching *Bed of Roses* with her, I struggled to come up with some tangible examples of my being romantic. In fact, I couldn't think of even one example. However, she put me on the spot, and there was no way I could just drop the conversation and watch SportsCenter.

I sort of got off the hook when I told her two things: 1) It's a scripted Hollywood movie and, I'm sorry, but nobody is that romantic on a regular basis, and 2) Christian Slater, her new King of Romance, had twice been arrested, once for allegedly beating his girlfriend while he was drunk and stoned, and a second time for groping a woman while he was drunk. How's that for romance?

This is yet another reason for having The Other Woman live with you and your wife for a short while. Every so often your wife will be in the mood for a romance movie and if The Other Woman is around, you can easily sneak off to do your own thing while the two ladies share a box of tissue while watching the flick.

Now back to reality: The fact is your wife will want to watch chick flicks every so often, and she will want to cuddle with you while watching, so it's probably in your best interest to do just that when there's no way to get out of it, which is inevitable.

To give you yet another assist, I'm including the below list of classic chick flicks your wife will likely gush over. If she leaves it up to you to choose the flick, select one from this list, and you'll score major points for the rest of the week. Here are the classic sappy romance films your wife will love (if she doesn't already):

- *An Officer and a Gentleman*
- *Beaches*
- *Before Midnight*
- *Before Sunrise*
- *Breakfast at Tiffany's*
- *Hope Floats*
- *Love Story*
- *Message in a Bottle*
- *Must Love Dogs*
- *Notting Hill*
- *Pretty Woman*
- *Shakespeare in Love*
- *Shall We Dance*
- *Sleepless in Seattle*
- *The Bridges of Madison County*
- *The English Patient*
- *The Notebook*
- *The Wedding Planner*
- *The Wedding Singer*
- *While You Were Sleeping*
- *You've Got Mail*

While you may have little interest in watching romance movies, if your back is up against the wall and your wife really wants you to watch a love story with her, tell her that if you're going to watch the chick flick with her, there has to be a quid pro quo. If you are going to watch one of her love stories, she's going to have to watch one of your guy movies with you. It's only fair that your wife sit through one of your favorite classics. She can even choose the flick (from your preapproved list, of course). To help you put the shoe on the other foot, here are some of the best classic guy movies of all time:

- *Animal House*
- *Back to School*
- *Caddyshack*
- *Die Hard*
- *Dirty Harry*
- *Fight Club*
- *First Blood (Rambo)*
- *Old School*
- *Point Break** (the original 1991 film)
- *Porky's*
- *Pulp Fiction*
- *Rambo II*
- *Road House**

- *Scarface*
- *Slap Shot*
- *Stripes*
- *Tango and Cash**
- *The Blues Brothers*
- *The Expendables*
- *The Godfather*
- *The Great Escape*
- *The Longest Yard* (the original, not the awful Adam Sandler remake)
- *The Terminator*
- *The Terminator II*
- *Vacation* (the original 1983 film)

---

* It is my opinion—and the opinion of several friends—that *Tango and Cash,* *Road House,* and *Point Break* all fall under the "Movies That Are so Incredibly Bad, They Are Good" category.

Hollywood figured out a long time ago that women love living vicariously through characters in romance films, and men love living vicariously through (and quoting) characters in action/adventure and comedy films. So what do you do when you and your wife are all set to watch a movie one night but you don't want to watch a romance film and she doesn't want to watch one of your favorite genres? Watch a good drama (e.g., a Tom Hanks film such as *Sully* or *Bridge of Spies*)—it's likely the perfect middle ground for you and her.

11.

Shopping: It's an Endurance Sport

"Marriage is neither heaven nor
hell, it is simply purgatory."
—ABRAHAM LINCOLN

The Iron Man World Championship triathlon held every year in Hawaii is considered by many to be the most physically and mentally taxing endurance sport in the world. According to the event organizers, the "140.6-mile journey presents the ultimate test of body, mind and spirit."

If the winner of the Iron Man really wants to impress me with his endurance, I would like to see him spend a day shopping with my wife. Now *that* is a true physical and mental challenge. When it comes to shopping with your wife, view it as if you were competing in the Iron Man triathlon—you are in for a very long, very trying, mentally and physically exhausting day.

There's just something about shopping that resonates with and draws in most women the way Florida resonates with and draws in the elderly. Consider this: The average sixty-three-year-old woman has spent eight years of her life shopping, according to a study done by GE Money. The researchers also found that the average American woman shops for 399 hours and 46 minutes each year—I know I'm stating the obvious, but that's more than one hour for each day of the year.

Men and shopping just don't mesh. Two days before Christmas in 2013 Yahoo! featured a series of photos titled, "Miserable Men of Instagram Photos Show Dark Side of Holiday Shopping." The men in the photos—many slumped over in chairs surrounded by shopping bags—looked, well, absolutely miserable.

A lot of wives, on the other hand, view shopping like an extreme endurance sport. They get psyched and pumped up to go shopping during the big sale at their favorite stores. Shopping can be, and often is, an all-day outing for them. Think of it the same way as when you play golf with your buddies. On the golf course, you try to familiarize yourself with the subtle nuances and quirks of all 18 holes. Our wives approach shopping the same way; they know every inch of the stores they shop in—they know where the figurative sand traps and water hazards are and how to avoid them.

Early on in our marriage, I used to accompany Lissette on most of her shopping expeditions. During that time—especially if we were shopping for clothes or shoes for her, which accounted for the overwhelming majority of our trips to the stores—I would follow her around like an obedient puppy. I know it's pathetic, but I came to accept it, and there were always other pathetic puppies in the stores.

One of the first shopping outings I had with Lissette was a harbinger of things to come. We were in a department store and she was looking for new shoes. Lissette probably tried on about fifteen pairs of dress shoes, while I patiently waited for her to make her choice. It's not like Lissette was looking at dress shoes, casual shoes, and perhaps a pair of sneakers; I'm talking about fifteen pairs of dress shoes that, to me, looked virtually identical.

After about thirty minutes, she narrowed her selection down to five different pairs. Getting impatient, I asked her, "Which pair of shoes are you going to buy?"

She looked at me and, without hesitation, said, "All of them."

I was dumfounded. I had maybe—maybe—bought five pairs of shoes (and I mean different types of shoes such as dress shoes, sneakers, hiking boots, etc.) in five years, and she, in one fell swoop, equaled that. If there were a 12-step program for shoe addicts, my wife would be a lifetime member.

As with the 10 Fatal Words with regard to birthdays, there are 8 Fatal Words with regard to shopping for clothing. Now don't get rattled; this is *not* another test that she will spring on you. In fact, the 8 Fatal Words aren't even directed at you—they are directed at the salesperson helping her out. Here they are: "Can you start a dressing room for me?"

When you hear these 8 Fatal Words, be prepared because you are going to be in that store for the long haul. I start my car every morning; I start exercising about the same time every day; and I start watching SportsCenter at about 10:00 every evening. Until I went shopping with my wife, I had no idea that you could "start" a dressing room.

As a guy who most likely is retail-challenged, you know that the few times a year when you shop for clothes by yourself you will go to the fitting room and ask the fitting room attendant if you can "try these on." "These" are usually a shirt or two and a pair of pants. You know that rarely will you ever take more than three or four items into a dressing room. It's just not natural for a guy to walk into a dressing room with a heaping pile of clothes, is it?

With women, it's markedly different. My wife negotiates her way through her favorite boutique stores much like Tom Brady leads the New England Patriots down the field at crunch time. Much like a professional athlete who takes the field, Lissette is in the zone as soon as we walk into the store—and *nothing* distracts her. She is unflappable. She is intently focused on the job at hand, which is to buy clothes. She also reminds me of Arnold Schwarzenegger's *Terminator* character as she stalks through the aisles. Just like the Terminator, she has the ability to quickly scan items from a distance and ascertain key data such as price, size, and material. It's quite a gift she has.

There literally have been times when the three of us—my wife, the salesperson helping her, and I—carry clothes to the dressing room that has been started for her. We create a makeshift assembly line, and once the clothes make it inside the dressing room, I'm left sitting there twiddling my thumbs as Lissette tries on the dozen or more items she has selected. At least I'm not alone because, as I mentioned, there always is one or two other obedient puppies waiting outside the fitting rooms.

Now the inexperienced men reading this are likely saying to themselves, *The hell with that. I'll just wander around while she's in there trying on her outfits.* Wrong. Do you really think your wife will let you run off while she's trying on new clothes? Believe it or not, while she's considering which outfits to purchase, your wife will want your opinion and will ask you such questions as, "Does this color work for me?" or "Isn't this dress so cute?" or "Can I get away with wearing this outfit to work?" As if you have any idea. It's like you asking her if she thinks the 3-4 defense is better against the run or the pass.

Here's a story that illustrates the perfect example of what my wife, your wife, and perhaps every wife on the planet wants to hear while they are clothes shopping: On one of our trips to Rhode Island, my wife took me into a boutique clothing store, and after about fifteen minutes, I was getting bored. It was a small store, and as my wife was modeling a shawl (which is basically an oversized scarf), another shopper said to her, "Oh, that's so cute on you." My wife, thrilled that this woman was actually paying attention, quickly turned away from me, looked at her, and said, "Thanks. I just love the versatility of it."

What the hell does that mean? *Versatility?* They

were talking about a clothing item that didn't have any sleeves.

I could live to be 100 years old and if my wife were to drag me into 500 clothing stores in our lifetime, I know that I will never—and I mean never—have a conversation with Lissette like that woman had with her in that store. Be that as it may, my wife heard exactly what she wanted to hear that day, and she ended up buying two shawls.

Let's set aside what your wife wants to hear for this brief but important warning: inevitably, while modeling clothes, your wife will ask you, "Does this outfit make me look fat?" When you hear this question, immediately, and I mean immediately, say, "Absolutely not, honey." Do. Not. Hesitate. Even if she does look a bit portly, don't even think about saying yes. If you pause or take time to think about it, it's too late. Once you hesitate, it's the same thing as saying, "Well, I can really see your love handles through that dress." Do not respond to this question either by saying something like, "Compared to what?" or "Well, you're really not as thin as you used to be." If you want to avoid your wife's possible meltdown in the store, tell her she looks great—even if you have to lie.

There have been several times when we were in a store that also sells men's clothes and my wife told the salesperson that she would like a dressing room started for me as well. It's like Lissette and the salesperson are in cahoots, and they *start* a dressing room for me whether I like it or not. My wife would tell me that it's time that I update my wardrobe, and the salesperson, looking me over, quickly agrees with her. I really don't have much say in the matter, and before I know it, my dressing room has been "started," and I'm in there trying on the various shirts, pants, and sweaters that she and the salesperson have picked out for me.

Even though Lissette knows I hate shopping for clothes, she will say to me something like, "The longer you complain, the longer we are going to be in the store." Although, I must admit that my wife has much better taste than I do when it comes to clothes (and everything else for that matter) and because of her sense of style and aesthetics, I do dress a lot better than when I was single.

One of the most grueling shopping excursions I went on with my wife was to Target. Yes, Target. Two excruciating hours in Target. We went there with a small shopping list of items (toothpaste, paper towels, and cereal, among a few other things). However, and I should have known better, Lissette can never go to a store for just a few things.

Well, what made this particular trip exceedingly exhausting for me was that I was on crutches as a result of having broken my leg in a bike accident about seven weeks earlier. If you think two hours of shopping under normal conditions is tough, try doing it while precariously maneuvering around shopping carts and down the aisles on crutches and wearing a walking boot. After two hours, I felt like I had gone through four thirty-minute boot camp workouts. When we finally left the store, I literally was spent and collapsed into the passenger seat of our car.

Although I wrote this book to give marriage advice and guidance to clueless men, here are some suggestions for women's clothing store owners that I believe could double store sales. Knowing that women are going to drag their husbands or boyfriends to the store—and that this experience is about as exciting as watching paint dry—here are some simple pointers for store owners to follow if they want to keep women (and men) in their store longer:

1. Get some big, comfortable recliners so guys can relax while their wives are shopping. If we're going to be bored, we at least want to be comfortable.

2. Instead of having the usual magazines such as *Vogue, InStyle,* and *Mademoiselle* that by default men find themselves thumbing through while their wives try on outfit after endless outfit, have such magazines as *Sports Illustrated, ESPN The Magazine, Motor Trend,* and *Men's Journal* available.

3. Install a big-screen TV and have it tuned to ESPN or a FOX Sports channel. Also provide free WiFi. Taking the concept even further, get a liquor license and have a keg of beer on tap. Food is also an important element of this equation, so allow the guys to order pizza and wings.

4. Install sleep pods. I've already said it—shopping with a woman can be exhausting. Some guys (and I include myself in this group) would like nothing better than to take a nap, especially if it's mid afternoon (around 2 or 3 p.m.), while their wives shop. After

a 30-minute power nap in a sleep pod, we would be energized and ready to take on the next three or four stores.

Even though you want to sell the clothes to women, you want to sell the in-store *experience* to men. If you cater to men's needs—the need to be entertained or at the very minimum the need to be comfortable—they will be content in your store for hours while their wives blissfully shop away. Hell, guys will want to go back to your store with their wives every weekend. I have yet to be in a women's store that has figured this out. Heed this advice, and you will probably see a significant spike in sales. You will also make millions of men who go shopping with their wives happy.

12.

Who Are You?

"A married man should forget his mistakes;
no use two people remembering the same thing."

—ANONYMOUS

If you and your wife are newlyweds, I'm going to assume that, like most couples, you have known each other for several years. I'm guessing that you probably dated for a few years and were engaged for perhaps a year or so.

Your wife, the love of your life, knows you as well—or probably better—than anyone. She knows what makes you happy. She knows what makes you mad. She knows the inner visceral you, the one that only she gets to see every day and every night. No one knows you like she does. Be that as it may, there will be a time in the future when your wife will tell you that she just doesn't know who you are anymore. How in the world could that be? How could the woman who is your soul mate suddenly, from out of nowhere, not know you?

Well, your wife will be struck with temporary

amnesia because of something you will do. You see, sooner or later, like I have done, you are going to do something that, in her opinion, is so asinine and so dimwitted that perhaps during a heated argument she will emphatically say to you, "You know, sometimes I just don't know who you are anymore!"

I have heard this from my wife, and virtually all of my married friends' wives have experienced temporary amnesia as well. It's only a matter of time until you do something that will trigger the same response from your wife. Just accept it. You know that you just can't help yourself, and as a guy, sooner or later you will do something so idiotic that your wife will pop a gasket and will want to distance herself from you pronto.

After you hear the "I don't know who you are" line from your wife—try as you might—there's no plausible way for you to defend your idiocy. As a matter of fact, don't even try to defend yourself because you'll likely only dig yourself into a deeper hole as you try to rationalize your idiotic behavior.

The first time I heard the "I just don't know who you are!" line from my wife was in 1999 when my brother-in-law Briayan (Lissette's only brother) turned twenty-one. Briayan's birthday is in mid-December, and at that time, he was a student at a local university. As you know, when you're in college, December means final exams time. Thus, Briayan was knee-deep studying for his finals. Despite that little fact, along with my brothers Dino and Chris, we decided we wanted to take him to Las Vegas for the weekend to celebrate his twenty-first. We figured it was only one weekend and he could study for his finals in the car, which is about a nine- to ten-hour round trip. I neglected to run this idea by Lissette.

When I called Briayan to tell him that we were going to treat him to a weekend in Vegas, he resisted and I pressured him. He kept resisting, and I kept pressuring him, telling him that we would have a great time. "Don't worry about studying," I said. "You'll have plenty of time to do that in the car."

Just as he was about to acquiesce, my wife walked into the room and asked me who I was speaking with. I took the phone from my ear and told her it was her brother, filled her in on our plan, and how I was just about to get Briayan to cave.

That was when she let me have it. "You're what?!" she asked me. Now, my wife isn't a yeller, but on this particular day, I think I saw steam coming from her ears. "He has three final exams next week! What in the world are you thinking?" Lissette continued to tell me in great detail what a foolish idea it was to take her brother to Las Vegas.

As I was standing there holding the phone, she started to walk away. Just as I was about to tell Briayan (who clearly heard his sister over the phone) our Vegas trip was off, Lissette stopped and turned back to me and said, "You know, sometimes I just don't know who you are anymore!"

I opened my mouth to say something to her but nothing came out. I then turned my attention back to Briayan, who I had left hanging on the phone. I asked him, "Are you still there?"

He said, "We're not going to Vegas, are we?" and I said, "We're not going to Vegas."

I hung up the phone, and with my wife decompressing in our bedroom, I didn't know what to do. Should I go in and apologize? Should I watch TV? Should I go for a walk? In hindsight, I guess trying to force a college student to go to Las Vegas while he was studying for final exams was a pretty stupid idea. (What is not surprising is that I wasn't alone in this particularly bad idea, as two other married guys—my brothers—wholeheartedly supported the idea of a Vegas trip.)

Soon after you hear, "I just don't know who you are" from your wife, she will retreat to a corner of the house as far away from you as possible. This is her cooling down period, and it could range anywhere from fifteen minutes to an hour, depending on the scope of your stupidity.

Like I said, there's no plausible way for you to explain and/or defend your idiocy, so stay away from her during this cooling down period. I repeat: Do not go near her or talk to her while she is cooling down; you'll only make matters worse. She wants and needs the quiet time to decompress and fully digest the scope of your asinine behavior. Go wash your car or clean your garage during her cooling down time.

When you feel that it's safe to reengage her, walk slowly up to your wife, apologize, and say something like, "I'm sorry for being an idiot and doing something so stupid." Just in case she still "doesn't know who you are," remind her that you are the guy that she fell in love with and married.

Admitting that you did something stupid will help validate her response to your behavior. While she may initially respond with a lecture and tell you to "think before doing something," once she gets her point across, she will forgive you until you commit your next asinine act.

13.

The "It's Fine" Zone

"In my house I'm the boss,
my wife is just the decision maker."

—WOODY ALLEN

Once you get married—actually once you get engaged—you will quickly find yourself in a position of having to provide your point of view and perspective on seemingly dozens of items and issues to which you have never given a first or second thought. Suddenly, and with little warning, you are going to have to activate a part of your brain that likely has been dormant since birth. The reason you will have to activate this part of your brain is because your wife will challenge you on a regular basis with these four simple words: "What do you think?"

Okay, you're probably thinking, *I've been asked "What do you think?" about various things since I was a kid, and it's never been a problem.* Sure, you've been asked, "What do you think?" about things that *you* think about on a fairly regular basis—things like cars, food, beer, sports, investing, and vacation destinations, to name a few. The "What do you think?" question from your wife transcends the issues you are so familiar with and requires you to enter into a new zone that I like to call the *"It's Fine" Zone.* As long as you are married, once you enter the "It's Fine" Zone, there's no turning back.

I remember the first time I entered this zone. My wife and I had been engaged for a few months and were in the process of planning our wedding. We were at a "wedding" store, and Lissette was looking at sample wedding invitations with the woman who was assisting us. The ladies were going on and on about the different colors, sizes, shapes, and even the font types of the sample invitations. Suddenly, my wife, with a few sample wedding invitations in her hands, turned to me and asked, "Bobby, what do you think?"

Mind you, I had never, not once in my thirty years leading up to that moment, been asked my opinion about a formal invitation.

Lissette handed me one of the invitations. I looked at it, and she again asked me, "So, what do you think?"

I looked at her and said, "I think it's fine, honey."

She then handed me another invitation and asked me, "What do you think about this one?"

I looked at it, then looked at her and said, "I think it's fine as well."

She then handed me a third sample invitation and asked, "What do you think of this one?"

I looked at it, then looked at her and said, "It's fine, too."

Truth be told, all of the invitations she showed me looked pretty much the same to me, and while we were going through this little exercise, I was thinking two things: 1) It's just an invitation, and 2) The people who receive the invitation are going to take a quick look at it, mark the wedding date down on a calendar, and probably toss it shortly thereafter.

The woman helping Lissette gave her a look as if to say, "That's how all the guys who come in here respond." Lissette said, "Okay," and they quickly resumed their conversation as if I wasn't in the room. Later that day, Lissette said she had wanted me to provide more input on the invitation. I told her—and this is the truth—that I trusted her judgment on such things much more than my judgment to make the right decision. If memory serves me correctly, she absorbed what I said and said, "You're right."

At that particular moment, I entered the "It's Fine" Zone, and I've been a frequent visitor ever since, having been asked by my wife over the years to provide feedback on countless items and issues that had never before registered or resonated with me. In the ensuing years since my initial visit to the "It's Fine" Zone, I have learned that women analyze, evaluate, and scrutinize commonplace items such as party invitations and silverware the way NFL quarterbacks study game film.

Because you will probably never have a strong interest in these routine items—coupled with the fact that your wife will almost always make the final decision—I recommend that when she first springs the "What do you think?" question on you concerning something such as a curtain or bedspread, respond to her by saying, "Honey, I think it's fine." Then, like I did years ago, you will have officially entered the "It's Fine" Zone. It's not that I am completely ambivalent to these items; it's just that after several years of marriage, I know with absolute certainty that Lissette always makes the right decision. Over the years, as you're out and about (translation: shopping) with your wife, you will build your list of items to which "It's fine" applies virtually all the time. This list will register with your wife, and when you're in a store with her and she's picking out that "adorable" new soap dish, she'll turn to you and say, "This is fine, right?"

To help you develop your list, I am sharing with you my "It's Fine" Zone list. Whenever my wife asks me my opinion about one of the items on this list, I typically give her the standard "It's fine, honey. Whatever you think is best," response. I believe the "It's Fine" Zone is the perfect middle ground for satisfying your wife's interests and questions and you not having any idea what you're talking about.

Bob's "It's Fine" Zone items:

- Area rugs
- Bedsheets
- China (not country)
- Crystal
- Curtains
- Decorative pillows
- Face towels
- Floor lamps
- Guest soap
- Guest towels
- Hand towels
- Holiday cards
- Household furniture (with the exception of the TV)

- Placemats
- Pots/pans
- Salad bowls
- Shower curtains
- Silverware
- Soap dishes
- Tablecloths
- Table lamps
- Wall sconces
- Wineglasses

Be forewarned: Never use *It's fine* to describe how your wife's new hairstyle looks. There's little to no upside in doing so.

Now, just because "It's fine" works for me (my wife got used to that response years ago, plus she knows I am always going to default to her on such decisions), it may not work for you—especially early on in your marriage. If you repeatedly say, "It's fine, honey" to your wife when she asks your opinion (even if you know she will make the final decision), it might drive her crazy. To avoid a possible meltdown from her, muster up some enthusiasm for whatever it is she is asking your opinion about and say, "That's great, honey." Even if it's not 100 percent sincere, she will appreciate your being "present in the moment."

14.

Going Out of Town? Make a List and (Have Her) Check It Twice

"Do you know what it means to come home at
night to a woman who'll give you a little love,
a little affection, a little tenderness? It means
you're in the wrong house, that's what it means."

—GEORGE BURNS

Over a Fourth of July weekend several years ago, close friends of ours got married in Carmel, California. It was one of the best weddings Lissette and I had ever attended because the newlyweds really went out of their way for their guests and made the occasion a three-day event. The evening before the wedding ceremony, they had a barbecue on the beach and the day after the wedding, they had an outdoor brunch at a country club overlooking Carmel Valley. Class acts all the way.

Before we left for Carmel, the groom (a good friend of mine) told me that it would be a "casual" weekend and that I didn't have to wear a suit and tie to the wedding. I was thrilled to hear this because I loathe wearing ties, especially on weekends. Well, I neglected to share all of the details of my conversation with the groom with my wife, and I packed clothes I thought were appropriate for the wedding. (The keyword in the previous sentence is "appropriate.")

Most of the time, my idea of appropriate clothes and my wife's idea of appropriate clothes for a social gathering are at the opposite ends of the clothing spectrum. I always err on the side of being underdressed, and Lissette always errs on the side of being overdressed.

I can't tell you how many times when I get dressed (remember, we get dressed in different rooms because my clothes are in a guestroom closet) in what I think are appropriate clothes and walk into our bedroom to show my wife my outfit, she says to me, "You are not going to wear that. Please go put on something that's appropriate for the occasion." I've been having wardrobe malfunctions long before Janet Jackson had hers at a Super Bowl halftime performance.

On the day of the wedding, less than an hour before the ceremony, my wife and I were in our hotel room getting dressed, and that's when I showed her what I had brought with me to wear. I was about to iron my shirt when Lissette said, "You are not wearing that shirt to the wedding."

I, of course, said, "Why not?"

Lissette didn't even hesitate with her reply: "That shirt does not go with that suit. It's not appropriate to wear it without a tie, and furthermore, you'll look like a busboy! You're not going to wear it."

In response, I said, "But Seth (the groom) said it was—"

"I don't care what he said," she said, cutting me off. "You are not going to wear that shirt and that's that."

I tried to argue my case, but I didn't get anywhere.

So there we were, about forty-five minutes from the wedding ceremony, and I'm sitting on the bed in our hotel room in my T-shirt without an appropriate shirt for the wedding. My wife, who was putting on her makeup in the bathroom, would every now and then holler something at me like, "I can't believe you thought that outfit was appropriate," or "I can't believe that after all these years I still have to tell you what's okay to wear and to not wear."

Well, the clock was ticking, and I was sitting there wondering what the hell I was going to wear to this wedding. About thirty minutes before the wedding was to start (the ceremony location was about a 15-minute drive from our hotel), I asked my wife, "What are we going to do?"

Her answer: "We're going to the men's clothing store down the street to buy an appropriate shirt for you."

Fortunately, earlier that day, while we were on our way to lunch, we walked by a boutique men's clothing store that was about three or four blocks from our hotel. We rushed into the store and found an "appropriate" shirt for me to wear and off we went to the wedding, which we made with about five minutes to spare. Unfortunately, that was not our last unplanned trip to said men's clothing store that weekend.

The following day, as I was putting on the shirt I was planning to wear to the after-wedding brunch (not the same shirt that I was barred from wearing to the wedding), my wife, with a disgusted tone in her voice and an even more disgusted look on her face, said, "Please tell me you are not planning on wearing that shirt to the brunch."

Here we go again.

If the shirt I had initially selected to wear for the wedding ceremony wasn't appropriate, the shirt I selected for the brunch was, according to my wife, even worse. I tried to tell Lissette again that the groom said it was a casual weekend, but she was beside herself.

Off we went to the boutique men's clothing store. The brunch, which was about twenty minutes away, started at 10:00 a.m., and as you may know, most stores, especially clothing stores, don't open until 10:00 on Sundays. So, at 9:55 we found ourselves standing in front of the same clothing store we went to the evening before. While we were waiting for the saleswoman to open the doors to the store, Lissette let out a long (loud) sigh, looked at me with utter disbelief, and said, "You know, sometimes you exhaust me!"

She then told me that, going forward, whenever we have to go to an out-of-town wedding, she would have to review and bless my outfits before we left our house. How could I argue with her?

We were (I was) lucky to be staying in an area that weekend with a men's clothing store nearby. I can only imagine how the weekend would have gone otherwise. Not good. So, I suggest if a friend invites you and your wife to an out-of-town wedding, show your wife your outfits *before* you leave home. It will save you and her a lot of aggravation.

15.

Basic Training

"We've just marked our tenth wedding
anniversary on the calendar and threw darts at it."

—PHYLLIS DILLER

Ever since I got married, I have had quite a few women say the same thing to me time and time again. They usually will say this one thing to me after I notice something about them that just doesn't register with single guys. For example, I may notice a woman's new hairstyle and pay her a compliment, or I may tell a woman that she looks good in the color periwinkle (it's a purple/bluish color). While they all thank me for the compliment, after a brief pause, they also say something like, "You've been trained very well by your wife."

The sad reality is that like most married men, yes, I have been "trained" by my wife. As you have likely gathered by now, thanks to my wife's influence, I am a more sensitive, observant, and gracious person than I was when I was single. My mom taught me manners, and Lissette has been teaching me how to be a better all-around person.

Lissette is a stickler for appropriate etiquette, appearance, and behavior. Being a woman, she naturally is much more adept than I am at all things deemed socially appropriate. But what separates my wife from the pack is her steadfast belief in her Hispanic culture, which for all intents and purposes has very high standards of social appropriateness.

In the first year that Lissette and I dated, we took a trip with her family to Guatemala. Prior to the trip, one of the things Lissette told me was that I would have to wear only collared shirts in Guatemala City, but I could wear T-shirts in the countryside.

Why, you may ask, was I banned from wearing T-shirts in Guatemala City? Because, I was told, wearing a T-shirt in the city is not considered appropriate. I mean, here we were in a developing country in scorching heat, but I couldn't wear a T-shirt in the city. It's the first and only time in my life that my attire was restricted to a city's boundaries.

Unlike the military, marital basic training isn't so much an event or series of events as it is an ongoing cognitive exercise. In place of obstacle courses and sleep deprivation that the military uses in basic training, you will receive constant reminders from your wife about what's appropriate and what's not appropriate. She will drill these into your head the way a drill sergeant orders a recruit to "give me twenty!"

As a single guy, what you have to understand is that a lot of women look at the man they intend to marry, and while they obviously see a person of the opposite sex, they also see what is tantamount to a fixer-upper house.

Several years ago, Lissette used to watch HBO's hit show *Sex and the City,* and on occasion, I would watch it with her. Don't judge me for it; in many ways, the ladies on *Sex and the City* were like dudes, especially Kim Cattrall's character Samantha. Anyway, I remember one episode when Samantha said to Carrie (Sarah Jessica Parker) that she was dating a new guy and that she was going to "Take him out shopping for a new wardrobe. He's like my cute little fixer upper."

Like she does with a fixer-upper house, your future wife sees tremendous potential and pictures in her head of how the house (aka you) will shape up and what it will look like in a few years after she takes charge and applies her finishing touch. Renee Zellweger's character Dorothy summed it up well when she said about Jerry (Tom Cruise's character) in *Jerry Maguire,* "I love him for the man that he is, that man that he almost is, and the man that I know he can be." She apparently wasn't totally satisfied with "the man that he is."

While you may initially try to resist your wife's ambitions to create a new-and-improved you, it will only be a matter of time before you realize that it's easier to go along with her strategy than to fight it.

I was first exposed to such training a few years before I got married. I had a fraternity brother in college who embodied all of the character traits of John Belushi's character Bluto in *Animal House.* This guy defined party animal. He drank almost every night and ended up in more trouble with campus security than just about every guy in our fraternity combined. At the beginning of our senior year, he began dating a woman and they eventually married. Well, about two years after we graduated, I ran into him at a mutual friend's wedding. To say that he went through a metamorphosis is an understatement. If there ever was a guy who needed basic training from a woman, he was it; his wife had transformed him from Bluto to Mr. Rogers, right down to the cardigan sweater.

Here's a perfect example of what I'm talking about when it comes to marital basic training. I was once having lunch with colleagues at a restaurant; of the six of us, only two of us were guys—a single friend and me. When the waitress began bringing the meals to our table, my buddy was among the first to get his plate. He started to eat right away rather than wait for everyone at the table to receive their meals. Being a gym rat who loved pumping iron, he had an insatiable appetite. The plate was barely down before he sucked it up like a Hoover vacuum.

He could have ordered and eaten dessert before my meal even arrived, and I certainly wouldn't have cared. However, I did notice that the ladies who had been served were not eating until the last person's dish was placed on the table. They were staring at my friend as he obliviously devoured his meal.

"He just doesn't know any better," one whispered to the other.

"But Bob's not eating his meal yet," the other whispered back.

That's when a third woman pointed at my banded ring finger and said, "It's because of *that*." (Translation:

"Bob does know better because he has been properly trained by his wife.")

The degree to which your wife will train you depends on her tolerance level, as well as your own. Let's face it; you're probably always going to do things she considers inappropriate, rude, or unacceptable—or perhaps all three. Being guys, that's just who we are at times. However, the training you will receive from your wife will mitigate the frequency of your inappropriate actions, which, in turn, will keep her happy.

16

Candles:
The New Tupperware

"The secret of a happy marriage
remains a secret."

—HENRY YOUNGMAN

Over the years, Lissette and I have hosted many parties at our house. We've held birthday parties, anniversary parties, holiday parties, retirement parties, art parties, and even a coed baby shower. With the exception of the coed baby shower,* I looked forward to and enjoyed every party we've held for our family and friends. Naturally, given that the parties were at our house, I was a willingly present cohost.

A few years after we were married, Lissette decided to host a party at our home for an entirely new party genre. When she said that she wanted to have a party for about twenty to twenty-five people, I said, "Cool, just let me know when." However, when she told me what this particular party was for, I quickly made other

---

* Note to expectant women: Guys don't enjoy baby showers.

plans that would get me out of the house that night. What type of party could drive a man from his own house? *A candle party.*

I bet you didn't even know such as thing existed. Neither did I.

Candles are to many women in the twenty-first century what Tupperware was to women in the 1950s. Candles may not be as functional as Tupperware and you can't use them to store leftovers, but make no mistake, candles are as much a part of a married couple's home as a microwave oven and washer and dryer. Trying to understand what candles mean to your wife is like asking her to understand the comedic genius of the Three Stooges. She doesn't get the Stooges, and you won't get candles.

I had no idea candle parties existed, and I also had no idea what one celebrates, or does, at a candle party. The only times my mom broke out candles when I was growing up was to put them on a birthday cake or when there was a power outage.

Candles, I have since learned, have transcended their original purposes of giving light and setting a romantic atmosphere. They are, for all intents and purposes, decorative items that our wives cherish the way we cherish our power tools. However, unlike men who actually use their power tools, women rarely, if ever, use their most prized candles.

For candle parties like the one my wife hosted, there's actually a company that finds a host to throw the party and then it pounces on the women who attend to: 1) buy as many candles as possible, and 2) solicit women in attendance to host follow-up candle parties for their friends. Suffice it to say, there's no keg of beer on tap and there's not a ball game on the TV during a candle party.

Here's what happens—based on my wife's account —at a candle party. A woman demonstrates (I have no idea how you demonstrate a candle aside from lighting the wick) the myriad candles for "the season" and the women in attendance *ooh* and *ahh* at them. They then open up their checkbooks.

They also play games a la the games women play at showers. More than twenty women showed up at Lissette's candle party, and at the end of the night, the representative from the candle company had an order in her hands for more than $1,200 worth of candles— that's the price of a very nice LCD TV. What a racket.

The twisted irony with our wives and candles is that they rarely use most of the candles that dot the inside and outside of our homes. They seem to forget that just because a candle has a flowery or fruity scent and is shaped like a pear or flower, that it's still just a piece of wax with a wick down the middle. They become fixated with how "cute" or "adorable" the candles are, and they are displayed on fireplace mantles, bookshelves, nightstands, dining room tables, bathroom sinks, kitchen counters, and coffee tables to collect dust.

My brother Chris's wife has (at last count) forty-one candles of different shapes and sizes in their living room and dining room alone. I'm not kidding. Could you imagine how my sister-in-law Victoria would react if my brother wanted to put forty-one (or even twenty) items of his choosing in their house? If we lived in Fantasyland, he would be able to get away with decorating their house with photos of his favorite Red Sox and Patriots players. But this is the real world, and candles have kicked his and my stuff to the garage.

Here's the good news and bad news: My wife recently told me that candle parties are somewhat passé and have been replaced primarily by another party genre: jewelry/clothing parties. Whichever one of these parties your wife decides to throw, you'll want to hightail it out of your house for several hours the night of her all-girl soirée.

17

Why Are You Driving Like a Maniac?

"Women like silent men, they
think they're listening."

—ANONYMOUS

One of the few downsides of living in greater Los Angeles is dealing with never-ending freeway congestion. Heavy freeway traffic is to Los Angeles what rain is to Seattle. If you live here, it's a daily part of your life that you just come to accept (there is a little letup on Saturdays and Sundays). The greater LA area has four of the world's most-congested freeways. Basically, the 405, 5, 101, and 10 Freeways are giant parking lots.

Freeway traffic in Los Angeles is like an exact science. I've been driving the LA freeways for more than twenty-five years, and I know exactly where and when traffic will come to a grinding halt and where and when it will—at least temporarily—pick up.

One of my pet peeves is slow-moving things. Translated, I'm a very impatient guy—and nothing tests my patience like a bottleneck on the 405 Freeway or 110 Freeway, especially when it's noon on Saturday or I'm in a rush to get somewhere. However, there is one thing that makes me more tense and impatient than driving on the LA freeways when there's complete gridlock: driving on the congested LA freeways with my wife. In his stand-up routine, the late comedian George Carlin asked his audience, "Have you ever noticed when you're driving, anyone who's driving slower than you is an idiot, and anyone driving faster than you is a maniac?" My wife quite often puts me in the latter category.

Whether Lissette and I visit friends or go out to dinner, I drive about 99 out of 100 times. My getting behind the steering wheel and her riding shotgun is as natural as water being wet. Inevitably, whether we have a sixty-minute or twenty-minute drive, my wife eventually will blurt out at least one of three things: "Slow down!" or "Can't you see that everyone is braking?" or "Why are you driving like a maniac?"

And, of course, when we're in the car, she over-reacts to everything. If another car suddenly swerves into our lane, even if it's 90 feet in front of us while we're going only 25 miles per hour, or if Lissette sees brake lights from the cars half a mile ahead of us, she will let out a loud gasp that makes my heart skip about five beats. I constantly tell her that one of these days she's actually going to give me a heart attack while I'm behind the wheel and then she will really have something to worry about.

Being behind the wheel while your wife is riding shotgun is like going through driver's education all over again. She will tell you what you did wrong, why it was wrong, and to not repeat the same mistake. I sometimes feel like there's a "Student Driver" sign on my car when Lissette is in the passenger seat. When I'm driving my wife says things to me like, "There's a stop sign coming up." No kidding? Is that what that red octagonal sign with the word *STOP* is?

After talking with several other married men who also do the lion's share of the driving when they're with their wives, we have concluded that there are some universal traits concerning married women when they're in the passenger seat. Here they are:

o Their depth perception is inexplicably and irreparably skewed. For example, if something happens 80 to 90 feet in front of us while we're on the freeway, to our wives, it looks more like 15 to 20 feet and closing fast. To them, all objects in the front, back, and side of our cars definitely appear closer than they are.

o They think that we always drive too fast. Regardless of the time of day, the driving conditions, or the speed limit, if we pass more than five cars in a row before another car passes us, we are driving too fast and they will tell us to slow down. "We're not in a race," is a favorite expression of my wife and the wives of some friends. Once we slow down we still have to deal with their skewed depth perception.

o They treat our right arms like pincushions. When that car 80 feet in front of us swerves into our lane, our wives reach over with their left hand and dig their fingernails (even if they just recently were polished) into our respective right arms. My wife once came close to drawing blood.

While commuting on the LA freeways is about as enjoyable as oral surgery, there is one reprieve that makes the commute tolerable: the carpool lane. During rush hour, the carpool lane can reduce a sixty-minute commute to about forty-five minutes.

Several years ago, Lissette and I worked for the same company for about eighteen months, and one thing I most looked forward to was jumping in the carpool lane every morning and evening and zipping past the sloths in the other lanes. This exuberance didn't last. Within about a week or two, I quickly found that "Why are you driving like a maniac?" and "Can't you see that everyone is braking!" and "Slow down!" were about as frequent as the traffic reports every seven minutes.

I'm not saying that my wife and I didn't spend some quality time together during our commute. We spent the forty-five or so minutes each day making plans and talking about various issues, and some of the time was very productive. Be that as it may, had we continued to work in the same office and driven in the carpool lane every Monday through Friday, for Lissette's next birthday—eschewing everything I shared with you in the first chapter about getting your wife a birthday gift that has meaning—I would have given her a gift that would have made our commute more relaxing for both of us: a blindfold. That would have been the trick to the ultimate stress-free, husband-and-wife commute.

Even if you enjoy driving (and if you find your wife is like mine) years from now when autonomous cars are permitted on public roads, you may want to consider buying one. Even if you sit in the driver's seat and your wife sits shotgun, you can rest assured that any yelling or overreacting by her most likely will be directed at the car itself.

18.

Having the Boys Over

"I never knew what real happiness was until
I got married and by then it was too late."
—MAX KAUFFMAN

My wife and I purchased our first house in the summer of 1995, less than a year after we married. Our starter home had a small den with an easterly facing wall that was all windows and French doors that led to a small brick patio in the backyard. Because the back wall was all windows, the room got plenty of sunshine and natural light, which made it our favorite place to relax indoors. We didn't put up curtains because the room was in the back of the house, and there was no need for privacy.

The only problem with having a wall of windows was that the glare from the sun made it difficult to watch TV in the morning. This really wasn't an issue at first because my wife and I seldom watched TV in the morning. However, it became an issue about a month after we moved in when football season began.

With no curtains, I found myself watching football games at 10:00 a.m. on Sundays often under intense sunlight. Even though the glare from the sun would permeate the den, when I watched football games by myself, I just angled the TV set away from the glare and that solved the problem.

One Sunday I invited my brothers, Chris and Dino, and a friend who also grew up in New England over to watch a Patriots game. Of course, Lissette told me that I had to clean the house if I was to have guests over. I did a quick cleaning job and then went to the store to get some beer and food. Before the guys arrived, I tried to angle the TV set—this was before HDTVs—away from the glare of the sun so that all four of us could enjoy the game.

When I realized that the angle that best mitigated the glare just wouldn't allow all four of us to comfortably view the TV, I realized that instead of moving the TV, I should block the sun from coming into the room. I went to our laundry room and grabbed an old wool blanket, a hammer and some small nails and proceeded to nail the blanket up so that it covered the windows and blocked the sunlight from coming into the room. Bingo. Even though it was a Rube Goldberg job, I was very proud of my solution—that is, until my wife came home from church and saw the blanket hanging there.

When Lissette walked into the room, our conversation went something like this:

"What is that (the blanket) doing up there?" she asked.

I said, "It's just up there to block the sun so we can watch the game."

"Take it down," she said.

I said, "But it's blocking the sun from—"

And she said, "I don't care. Take it down. Do you think we live in a barn? How would you like it if we showed up at someone's house and they had a dirty old blanket hanging over their windows? Would you like that? You know your mother raised you better than that. I can't believe you. That's so random!"

I said, "I could care less if I showed up at a friend's house and he had an old blanket hanging there. Besides, it's my brothers, and they don't care if—"

And she said, "Well, I do care. Take it down now!"

Down came the damn blanket. I think we caught only about half the action of the game that day because of the glare on the TV.

Such is the conundrum of having the boys over when you're married. Most things that are readily acceptable to you and your friends will never be readily acceptable to your wife. Do any of your friends care if your house is a mess (and *mess* is a relative word) when they show up to watch a ball game? Hell no.

As a close friend has said time and time again, "The only thing that I care about when I come over to your house is that you have beer in the refrigerator and that the football game is on TV." I can guarantee you he's not looking for the guest soap.

Even though your guy friends don't care if the house is a pigsty, your wife will want it spick-and-span whenever you invite the boys over. It's like our wives are paranoid that our friends are going to run home and tell their wives that the house was unkempt. In fact, if the house was a mess, most guys would go home and probably say to their wives something like, "You know,

I don't know why you make such a big deal about having such a clean house when my friends come over. I was just at Bob's house, and it was a mess and his wife doesn't seem to mind."

My friend's theory is that women know that men hate cleaning the house. Furthermore, our definition of a clean house is vastly different from that of our wives. As such, whenever we want to have the boys over, the universal prerequisite from our wives is that we have to clean the house, and it has to be approved by the inspector (you know who this is).

He believes, and I agree with his theory, that virtually every married woman today strategically uses the "You know, if you're going to have your friends over you have to clean the house" line to dissuade their husbands from inviting the boys over. He figures that about half of married men faced with this dilemma simply say, "The hell with it," and end up watching the game alone or meeting their friends in a bar because they decided it was too much of a pain in the ass to clean their house.

In addition to hiring a good housekeeper, I recommend that if you do have the boys over to watch a football or baseball game, first put up nice new curtains. Of course, you could also do what my brother Chris did—he converted his garage into a so-called man cave, complete with a 55-inch LCD television and refrigerator. Although he has a TV in his den, when we get together at his house, we always watch the game on the TV in what was his garage, and his wife (who doesn't watch games with us) usually lets it slide if he hasn't cleaned the man cave.

19

You Need to Be More Emotional

"All marriages are happy, it's the living together afterwards that causes all the trouble."

—RAYMOND HULL

Several years ago Lissette and I attended a friend's wedding in Santa Barbara. The newlyweds held the ceremony and reception at a historic vineyard on the outskirts of the town, and it was one of the best weddings we've attended. The reception was held in a large old mission-style house, and when it was time for dinner, all the guests sat at tables elegantly arranged in an enormous wine cellar.

Just after the guests sat down for dinner, the groom stood up and thanked everyone for attending. He said that he and his wife were honored to have friends and family join them on their special day. About three or four minutes into his speech, while he was talking about the importance of being surrounded by family and friends, he got all choked up. He paused to gather himself, and then continued to speak, albeit while he was wiping away a few tears.

It was a touching moment, and as you can imagine virtually every woman in the room—including my wife—broke out some tissue and wiped their eyes. Just as he finished his remarks, my wife turned to me and said, "You see, you need to be more emotional." As if I had a label on my forehead that read "devoid of emotion," a woman—who was a complete stranger—sitting at our table overheard Lissette, looked at me, and said, "She's right, you know."

Later that evening, I approached the groom, and after congratulating him, I jokingly said, "That was a wonderful thing you said, but you made the rest of us guys look like shit with our wives." Wearing a crooked smile, he told me he was sorry.

Before I had kids, I was not what you would call a highly emotional person. While I was very happy and joyous, I didn't cry on my wedding day. There are some indelible moments that have caused me to tear up or get a lump in my throat. For example, I fell to my knees and cried like a baby when the Red Sox won the 2004 World Series. I mean after enduring years of heartbreak and agony, what true Red Sox fan didn't weep? (I even cried while watching the replay of the final out on my DVR several weeks after that World Series victory.) Needless to say, I was overcome with joy and unbridled emotion each time the Patriots won their five Super Bowl titles. Unfortunately, these emotional moments don't count one iota with my wife.

I once read an article on CNN's website about a

study from the State University of New York Stony Brook that proclaimed that women have more emotional states than men. The study claimed that women's brains are wired both to feel and recall emotions more keenly than the brains of men. What a breakthrough discovery. Are you kidding me? Seriously, the team of psychologists that conducted the study could have sat down with me or any of my married friends and would have come to that conclusion in fewer than five minutes. We would have spared them months of research and analysis.

Once married, your wife will want you to display a new range of emotions you don't even know exist in you. She will push you to reveal a side—no, make that multiple sides—of you that likely has been lying dormant since you were born. You know how some people, be they an athlete or musician, are just born with an abundance of natural talent? Well, virtually all women are born with an abundance of emotions, and you never really quite know which emotion will show up on a given day and how long your wife will be in that emotional state.

Your wife's emotional range is sort of like the stock market. Just like you never truly know if the market is going to be up or down from one day to the next, you will never really know which emotion will surface from your wife. And just like there often are extenuating circumstances—some of which make no sense and have no relevance whatsoever—that influence the market's performance, there are a multitude of factors that can affect your wife's emotions. You can't time the market and you can't time your wife's emotions, and sadly, there is no guru a la Warren Buffett whose advice you can heed when it comes to women's emotions.

Try as you might, you will probably never be able to register as high on the emotional scale defined by your wife. Now don't confuse being emotional with being affectionate. You could kiss and hug your wife every morning when you leave the house and every evening when you get home, but that doesn't mean you're an emotional guy.

Unlike her, you will not cry at sappy romance movies or at weddings or at any other social functions such as a baby's baptism. There's a woman I know who is so emotional that she once cried while watching a McDonald's commercial that featured little kids. I'm not kidding. We were at a Super Bowl party and she started crying during the McDonald's commercial that featured little kids doing something kids do. A crying woman is not who guys want to be around while watching the Super Bowl.

Given all of that, every now and then your wife will want you to display more emotion than you ever knew you were capable of mustering up. She will challenge you, and while at times it may feel as if you were being force fed, you'll have to reach down deep within yourself, tap that shallow reservoir of emotion, and find that one emotional bone in your body.

If your wife is prodding you to be more emotional and you can't exhibit the required emotion, then you risk upsetting her and that triggers perhaps the most volatile and dangerous female emotion: anger. She might say something to you like, "I can't believe I married such an insensitive person." Believe me, you don't want to see that emotion surface, so go ahead and tear up during that sentimental movie on Netflix that she will have you watch with her. Your friends will never know, and chances are their wives have already asked them to do the same thing.

While I have never cried watching what my wife considers a moving romantic film scene, I am a dog lover and a close friend of mine is as well, and we both admitted to tearing up while watching *Marley & Me*. He also told me his wife looked at him, handed him a tissue, and said, "It's okay," which is basically what Lissette did for me. *Marley & Me* actually made me tear up on two separate occasions: first while reading the book and later while watching the movie.

When you're married, showing your wife that you can be a more sensitive and emotional guy, even if it's only a handful of times a year, just comes with the territory.

20

"Cool Glasses"

"My wife and I were happy for
twenty years. Then we met."

—RODNEY DANGERFIELD

Several years ago, after having the same pair of eyeglasses for about three or four years, I decided that it was time to get a new pair of glasses. After my eye exam, I went to the optometry store and looked at the dozens of different frames on display. I was by myself, and although I was a bit overwhelmed by the wide selection of frames, I was determined to make the decision on my own and select a new pair of glasses without having to rely on my wife's input.

After about five minutes of trying on different frames, I narrowed down my selection to three pairs. They all looked pretty similar, so knowing that I would need the opinion of at least one female before I made my decision, I asked the young woman who was assisting me which pair of glasses she thought looked best on me. She told me that all three looked good and that I couldn't go wrong with any one of them.

I was just about to select the frame I had decided

on when the woman noticed my wedding ring and said, "You're married, right?"

Knowing exactly where she was going with this conversation, I said, "Yes, I am."

She then said, "You probably want to bring your wife into the store and see what she thinks. Most married men who buy their glasses here rely on their wives to select the frame that's best for them."

Trying to be coy, I said, "Really, that's interesting . . . I'll be back shortly."

As I headed out of the store, my steadfast determination to make my own decision left right behind me. Later that day, I returned to the optometry store with Lissette, and the young woman who had been helping me earlier in the day put the three frames I was considering on the counter. As if I wasn't even part of the decision-making process, the woman looked directly at Lissette and asked her, "What do you think?"

Without hesitation—without even giving me the opportunity to try them on—my wife looked at the three frames, pointed to them one by one, and said, "No, no, and no."

What you have to understand about my wife is that she eschews conventional style with virtually everything that she does. She's a nonconformist and her disdain for the ordinary applies to everything from her first car, which was a Saab, to the color of our house, which is painted deep dark terracotta, in a neighborhood of white, Navajo white, and eggshell white houses. She strives to be different from the masses and has her own distinct, eclectic style.

So Lissette decided that she was going to select a pair of glasses for me that were bold and made a statement. I've never been a make-a-statement type of guy. For about twenty minutes, my wife and the young lady took down from the display cases about fifteen different frames for me to try on.

I just sat there and watched the two of them go to town. As quickly as my wife said no to the three frames I was initially considering, I dismissed frame after frame she had me try on. She picked out a couple of frames that made Elvis Costello's large black-frame glasses look conservative. I was just about ready to call it quits and keep the pair of glasses I had been wearing for a few years, when Lissette handed me one last pair of glasses that she selected and asked me to try them on. Bingo!

Now, I'm not a very hip guy, but the first time people I know saw me with my new glasses, they said things like, "Those are very cool glasses" or "I really like your glasses" or "Hip glasses." Whenever I said thanks, I felt obligated to say, "My wife picked them out." Many people who know me and complimented me on the glasses of course asked with a hint of uncertainty in their voice, "Did you select them?" Even complete strangers complimented me on my new glasses. Not that I was looking for it, but I had never before received so many compliments on anything I had ever worn.

Therein lies one of the inherent advantages of being married—you have a year-round/live-in fashion consultant who has far superior and discriminating taste than you. Bloomingdale's ran a radio commercial during the holiday season a few years ago that featured a married woman waxing poetically about the clothes she was going to purchase as Christmas gifts for the members of her family. When the woman began speaking about her husband, the only thing she said was that she was looking forward to getting some new clothes for "My husband, who has a constant struggle with fashion." I think many married woman would echo that sentiment.

Practically every article of clothing I have was either selected by my wife or received her stamp of approval. A woman I once worked with told me that some of the ladies at the company considered me to be one of the best-dressed guys in the office. Not that I care about that, but after I thanked her, she said, "Of course, we know that your wife picks out your clothes." I couldn't argue with her—Lissette practically lays my clothes out for me each morning like my mom did when I was a kid getting ready for school.

I now work at home, but for years I worked in what could be described as typical corporate environments. When I worked in such offices, I often got up and dressed before Lissette awoke. I can recall countless times when I went into our room to give my wife a kiss good-bye, and even though she would be half asleep, she would look at me and groggily say, "That shirt doesn't go with those pants," or "You shouldn't be wearing that color and/or fabric this time of year." Even half asleep, she has a better sense of fashion than I do.

You're going to have to accept the fact that your wife may want to redefine your look and your style (if you even have any). Believe me, she knows what she's doing. Her inclination to do so is just like a mother bird going to get food for her hatchlings—the mother bird knows a hell of a lot better what's good for them, and she will leave them in the nest until they are ready to fly on their own.

21.

It's That Time of the Month (or Week)

"I've sometimes thought of marrying,
and then I've thought again."

—NOEL COWARD

It's no secret that women want and crave affection more than most men. They want to be hugged. They want to be kissed. They want to be touched. They want men to do little things like hold them during a romantic movie like the ones I listed earlier. My wife is no different, and over the years, I have come to understand and appreciate her need for more loving affection from me.

Every now and then—just to keep me on my toes—my wife will remind me that I need to be more affectionate. She'll say something like, "Why is it that I always have to ask you for a kiss?" I make a mental note of her comment, and I try to show her my more affectionate side. I try to kiss her more and I try to hug her more.

Lissette isn't big on flowers, so instead of bringing home a dozen red roses, every so often I'll bring her a card with a black-and-white photo of babies dressed like adults, and I'll write her a note to let her know how much I love her.

While my wife wants me to show her more affection, there is a recurring time, about once a month, when she doesn't want me to even touch her. It doesn't last very long, but during this time, she might as well put up the yellow tape that police use to cordon off a crime scene around her to keep me away. I have found that most of my married friends experience the same thing with their wives.

What could happen once a month that makes my wife virtually completely forego her need for my affection? Now I know what you're thinking, and it's not that. In two words: fingernail polish. When my wife "does her nails," it's as if she's just been exposed to a Level 4 biohazard, and I can't go near her or touch her. And if you are familiar with the repugnant odor of fingernail polish, I wouldn't be surprised if it's considered a biohazard in some countries. The stuff stinks.

I don't even have to be in the same room with my wife, but I always know when it's that time of the month because while she is applying the fingernail polish the odor permeates the walls and I can smell it from the other side of our house. After the smell subsides, I'll take a chance and go into the room where she has been applying the polish, and she'll be sitting there as stiff as a board.

Immediately after my wife finishes applying the polish, she won't touch anything and nothing is allowed to touch her for at least forty-five minutes. If I try to lean in and give her a kiss, she won't say something like, "Thank you, that's so sweet." No, she'll immediately snap at me and say, "Please, honey . . . watch the nails!" During this time, Lissette treats her fingernails and toenails as if they were just dipped in gold.

There have been countless times right after my wife has done her fingernails when we were on our way out and I had to open the front door of our house, the passenger door of our car, and put her seatbelt on for her. Once I had to help her put on her pants, zip up her fly, and button her pants after she did her nails. It's like she's suddenly become royalty, and I'm her servant. She won't touch a damn thing right after she does her nails.

I know as much about nail polish as I know about the Parliament of Australia, which is to say, not much. I thought like my wife, most women applied nail polish (or had it applied at a salon) every 30 days or so. Wrong. Lissette works from home and is able to, in her words, "Get away with changing nail polish about once a month." According to my wife, most ladies have their nails done almost every week, so you may see this side of your wife more frequently.

Even if you are feeling amorous and want to shower your wife with affection and attention (something she probably usually appreciates), freshly applied nail polish can—at least temporarily—serve as a makeshift blockade and put the kibosh on those feelings. In fact, after your wife does her nails, don't be surprised if you become persona non grata for one or two hours.

22.

A Sixth (and Probably a Seventh) Sense

> "If variety is the spice of life, marriage
> is the big can of leftover Spam."
>
> —JOHNNY CARSON

Several years ago, when Lissette and I attended the wedding in Santa Barbara that I mentioned earlier, most of the guests we socialized with were my work colleagues—most of whom were married. However, one of my coworkers, a good friend, who also attended the wedding was a single guy that I used to live vicariously through.

This particular guy, who was in his midtwenties at the time, was a transplant from New York. As one of the few single guys in the office, his weekend escapades in Hollywood and elsewhere were legendary at work. Every Monday, I would call him into my office and he would tell me and a couple other married guys about the parties or bars he and his single buddies went to over the weekend. We loved living vicariously through him.

His date for the wedding was a young woman from our office whom he had been seeing for about two months. I had known this woman for about a year or so, and she seemed like a nice enough person. I thought they made a good couple. During the wedding reception, they sat at the same table as my wife and I and about three other couples. My wife didn't spend a lot of time chatting with my friend's date. In fact, during the course of the evening, they probably spent fewer than ten minutes talking with each other.

On the drive back to our hotel, I asked Lissette what she thought of her, and she said something like, "She's sweet and seems like a very nice person, but she's not right for him."

I said, "How could you possibly know that? You just met her and the two of you barely spoke."

For the next five minutes, my wife told me why she didn't think they were right for each other. I can't remember the specific details of our conversation, but she articulated her reasons for why the young lady wasn't right for my friend. About a week after the wedding, they broke up. My friend and I were having lunch, and he told me that she just wasn't who he thought she was and it just wasn't working out. I practically fell out of my chair.

That's when I started to truly comprehend the mystique and magical powers of my wife's intuition—and women's intuition in general. Over the years, I have learned and witnessed that my wife's intuition about a person or particular issue is dead-on accurate. Early on in our relationship, I dismissed her intuition as her

135

being critical and/or overly sensitive. Now, after seeing and experiencing the astounding aura of my wife's gut instinct, I never doubt her when she says she has a "certain" or "funny" feeling about someone or something.

A woman's brain is just wired different from a man's brain. I really don't know how they do it, but women like my wife pick up signals—signals that elude us men altogether—with the pinpoint accuracy of a smartphone's GPS. There doesn't seem to be a reasoning process involved. In my humble opinion, a woman's perception of the truth or facts (which readily escape a man) just can't be logically explained. When was the last time one of your guy friends said to you, "You know, I can't put my finger on it, but I have a funny feeling about (*fill in the blank*)?" Probably never. While puzzling, and many times even baffling, our wives' sixth sense is an intangible, yet highly powerful character trait that us guys will never possess.

Here is perhaps the best example of my wife's "super power." About sixteen years ago, my older brother, Dino, became engaged to a woman he met through my wife's family. Dino is one of the nicest guys in the world. While our family was very happy for my brother, soon after he became engaged, my wife told me that she had "concerns" and a "funny feeling" about the situation. I told her that she was crazy and that there was nothing to be concerned about.

Now before I go on, there's another thing you have to understand about my wife: she is the most caring, thoughtful, considerate, and accepting person I have ever met. Lissette is an idealist, and she believes that virtually all people are good and have good intentions, unless they prove otherwise. My wife gives her unconditional love to her family and friends, and has a way of even making strangers feel like family. To prove my point, seven of our friends asked Lissette to be godmother to their child. I don't know anyone else with that many godchildren. I even became godfather to some by association.

So, back to her intuition kicking in. Every now and then Dino would tell Lissette and me about how his wedding plans were coming along. Later—after we were alone—Lissette would confide in me that she still had misgivings. Again, I'd try to convince her that everything was okay.

Based on her amorphous feelings, my wife even tried to get me to talk to Dino about her concerns. "So, let me get this straight," I said. "You want me to tell my brother that he should think twice about going forward with this wedding because you have a funny feeling? Are you nuts?"

I wish I had listened to her.

That summer, my brother's fiancée and her mother (who lived in Central America) visited him in Los Angeles so they could discuss the wedding plans and purchase a wedding dress. That's when the proverbial shit hit the fan. In swift fashion, my brother's future mother-in-law systematically sabotaged the wedding plans. Within a few days of her visit, this woman decided, among other things, that she didn't like Dino's apartment or his car or how he "lived." She basically said she didn't think he was good enough for her daughter, and they would not be married. About a week later, my brother's fiancée called off the wedding.

Shortly after the kibosh was put on my brother's wedding, I asked Lissette how she knew that my brother's ex-fiancée and her mother were trouble. She looked at me and said, "I just had a funny feeling." Enough said. It was that heinous episode that firmly cemented my steadfast belief in my wife's intuition and sixth (and perhaps a seventh) sense. Lissette never said, "I told you so." That's just not her style. Following that episode, I told my wife two things: 1) I wish I had listened to her about speaking with my brother, and 2) I would never again doubt her when she expresses concerns or a "funny feeling" about someone or something.

One day sooner or later, your wife is going to tell you that she has a funny feeling or concerns about someone or something. While you may initially think she's been smoking weed and is suffering from smoke-induced paranoia, I strongly recommend that you take her concerns very seriously and remember the lesson I have shared with you.

23.

Pay Close Attention to Gay Men

> "'I am' is reportedly the shortest sentence
> in the English language. Could it be that
> 'I do' is the longest sentence?"
>
> —GEORGE CARLIN

One evening, not long after we were married, I was hanging around our apartment waiting for my wife to come back from wherever she had been. It was getting late and we were planning to meet friends for dinner so I jumped in the shower.

When Lissette got home, she came into the bathroom to let me know she was back. I opened the shower door and said hi, and then she said that she would be ready to leave in about thirty minutes. I said okay, but she just stood there. After about five to ten seconds or so of silence, she said, "Don't you notice anything?" It took me a few seconds, but then I realized that she looked different, so I said, "Oh, you got your hair cut." Then I closed the shower door and went back to showering.

When I got out of the shower, I found my wife in our bedroom getting dressed for dinner, and that's when she let me have it. "I can't believe that the only thing you can say about my new hairstyle is that I got my hair cut," she said.

"What should I say?" I asked.

She said, "Can't you compliment me on the way it looks or how it makes me look?"

So, not knowing that I was just digging myself an even deeper hole, I said, "It looks nice."

She then said, "*Nice.* Is that all you can say? You know, you are such a guy."

Translated, "You are such a guy," means that you are a person devoid of observation and stimuli. You are (in your wife's opinion) an overgrown child. All-pro NFL tight end Rob Gronkowski could be the "You are such a guy" poster child.

What my wife wanted to hear from me that day was something like, "Your new hairstyle looks fabulous. The way your hair is layered and falls on your face, well, it looks flawless and really works for you." Of course, no straight guy would ever say something like that even if he's been through basic training.

I have learned that married women want—make that *need*—their husbands to not just notice their new hairstyle or dress, they need us to be keenly observant and to reach deep within ourselves and come up with a sincere compliment that will make them feel warm inside.

So what's one of the best ways to learn to be more observant and shower your wife with compliments that she will soak up like a sponge? It's very simple: pay close attention to gay men when they hang out with your wife. Okay, let the politically correct cynics say I am making an insensitive generalization. Again, from personal experience, I don't think I am.

I can honestly say that you will learn how to be more observant by watching your wife interact with gay men. I'm dead serious. We have several gay friends, and gay men notice things on, and about, women that we straight guys barely ever notice. Gay men pick up on a woman's little things—let's call them accessories—that resonate with her. Why do you think women prefer to shop with gay men? First off, my gay male friends actually *enjoy* shopping. Also, our wives can count on gay men to tell them, for example, those shoes are "fabulous" and compliment her dress or purse or jewelry.

When Lissette is around our gay male friends, they notice things—things that don't even register with me—and compliment her on almost everything she's wearing. Here's a selective sampling of just a few of the things that our gay friends compliment her on: purses (this is a big one), earrings, shoes (another big one), bracelets, necklaces, nail polish color, scarves, lipstick color, and clothes. They will say things like, "That purse is *très chic*" or "Those shoes are fierce."

Our wives love to hear that stuff, be it from a gay man or from another woman, and every now and then, they also want to hear something complimentary from their husbands. Now don't think that you will have to tell your wife that her purse is "adorable." I've never said anything like that to my wife, and in my lifetime,

I have heard only one heterosexual man (who later divorced his wife and came out of the proverbial closet) say anything even remotely close to that to a woman.

To avoid the "you're such a guy" label, just make an effort to notice what she wants you to notice and compliment her on it. It's important to do so because a compliment from you can also—in your wife's mind—justify the ridiculous prices she sometimes pays for things like a haircut or pair of shoes.

24

Decisions, Decisions, Decisions

"A man's wife has more power over
him than the state has."

—RALPH WALDO EMERSON

A Los Angeles company once ran a commercial on local radio stations for several weeks during morning rush hour hawking its product or service that was brutally honest about a particular shortcoming of married men. I don't remember the name of the company; I can't even remember what the company was selling. However, I do remember the premise of the commercial, which was this: when it comes to making a decision without their wives' input, married men vacillate more than Donald Trump tweets.

The commercial was blatant in its portrayal of a married man as an indecisive boob, incapable of making a decision without approval from his wife. The guy in the commercial ruminates over and over until his wife steps in, cuts him off, and makes a decision. Sadly, the commercial rings true in more ways than one.

Not too long after you become a husband, you will eventually find that your ability to be decisive and make an independent decision has been compromised. It's not something that happens overnight. In fact, it may take a few years for your decision-making skills to deteriorate, so enjoy your decisive demeanor while it lasts. You may be thinking to yourself, *I'm my own man, and there's no way I'm going to cave in to my wife every time an important decision has to be made.*

It's not caving in to your wife and don't blame her if your decision-making skills begin to deteriorate. While your wife may change many things that will come to define you (such as your style of clothes), she will not try to undermine your decision-making ability on purpose. In fact, she will almost always solicit and want to hear your opinion concerning the topic of discussion at the time. But here's the rub: when you are faced with making a decision, it's not that you make the wrong decision; it's that your wife has developed a decision-making acumen that often is far superior to your ability to act decisively or make the right choice.

Over the years, you will come to accept your wife's superior decision-making ability, and as a result, you will naturally defer to her better judgment, regardless of the issue at hand. My wife has far—and I mean far—better judgment than I do. She just always seems to know what's best for our family. It's like she has a damn crystal ball that only works for her.

A wife's ability to make better decisions than her husband applies to everything from clothes to furniture and artwork in your home to the color of your car to birthday gifts for your friends and family members. My wife selects every gift that "we" give to friends and family. While I never know what to get for birthdays or holidays, Lissette has a natural affinity for deciding which gift is best for which person. There have been countless times when friends or colleagues thanked me for the gift I gave them, and I had no idea what the gift was until they opened it in front of me. After they thank me, I say, "I knew you would like it."

Selecting the right gifts is just scratching the surface of my wife's superior decision-making ability. While I may struggle at times to make certain decisions, Lissette has an innate ability to make the right choice and know what's best, regardless of the situation.

My father turned eighty-five in December 2016, and my brothers and I decided we would celebrate his birthday with a family dinner at a restaurant he enjoys near my home. When I made the reservation for sixteen people two weeks before my dad's birthday, the hostess at the restaurant told me that for a party that big it's best to make a set menu by selecting five or six entrees from their overall menu.

The restaurant's menu featured more than twenty dinner entrees. Suffice it to say, I was a bit overwhelmed by the choices, and while perusing the menu, I said to the hostess, "Boy, it's tough narrowing it down from so many choices." As I continued looking at the menu, she asked me, "Are you married?" I knew exactly where she was going with her question. I said yes and told her that I'd be back with my wife.

A few days later, I returned to the restaurant with

Lissette. The hostess handed the menu to my wife, and in about five minutes, Lissette selected the six entrees. It's not that I couldn't decide; it's just that I knew (and I guess the hostess also knew) that my wife, with her spot-on judgment, would make the right choices. The night of the birthday dinner, everyone (even my dad, who is incredibly picky when eating out) found something on the menu they liked.

The biggest downside to your wife's ability to make better decisions than you is that, eventually, when you have to make a decision without her (for example, if she's out of town), you may be somewhat plagued by self-doubt. Don't worry; that's natural. Just do your best. But if you can, hold off making that decision until she returns.

25

Victoria's Real Secret

"I never mind my wife having the last word.
In fact, I'm delighted when she gets to it."
—WALTER MATTHAU

It's no secret that virtually every guy who lives with a woman looks forward to the day the Victoria's Secret catalog arrives in the mail. I know you love your wife, but if the Victoria's Secret catalog arrives on the same day as *Sports Illustrated,* you're usually gonna toss SI on the coffee table to collect dust while you thumb through Victoria's Secret. Admit it, you probably know the first names of certain Victoria's Secret models as well as you know the players on your fantasy football team.

While you're still single, there's a good chance your girlfriend will order some sexy lingerie from this coveted catalog, and there's an even better chance that, every now and then, she will model the slinky, revealing undergarments for you. In the spring and summer, she will probably wear said lingerie to bed on a semi-regular basis.

Now, let me clue you in on Victoria's real secret (which has been corroborated by virtually all of my married guy friends): Once you get married, that sexy, slinky lingerie will end up in the same storage box as your wife's college yearbook. Kiss that sheer lace nightgown she wears to bed good-bye. This might not happen right away, but eventually, that sexy sleepwear will be replaced by T-shirts (that used to be yours), sweatshirts, boxer shorts, and pajamas with the built-in slippers such as Pajamagram's Hoodie-Footie that, according to the description on its website, is "specially designed to deliver head-to-toe warmth." My wife gets cold when the temperature drops below 70 degrees, so even though we live in Southern California, there are many nights when I get into bed with Lissette and the only parts of her body that aren't covered are her head and hands.

One of my married friends has a theory, which I think has merit: Single women wear sexy G-strings and thongs from Victoria's Secret because it comes with the territory of being single. They wear teeny-tiny underwear, even if it is as uncomfortable as wearing rubber bands, and tolerate it while they are dating. Why do they tolerate it? Quite simply, men find such sleepwear incredibly sexy and women know they do.

A single woman I know once admitted to a group of us who were hanging out that the lingerie from Victoria's Secret that she wears to bed at night is not at all comfortable and ends up around her neck by the time she wakes up in the morning—and that's without the proverbial roll in the hay. She also said she couldn't wait to get married so she could wear something more comfortable like a T-shirt and sweatpants to bed every night. So, there you have it, straight from the horse's mouth (no offense intended), so to speak.

26.

Pass on the Gas

"Marriage is not just spiritual communion,
it is also remembering to take out the trash."

—DR. JOYCE BROTHERS

A few years after my wife and I married, a coworker and close friend proposed to his girlfriend and she accepted. About three months before his wedding, he asked me, "As a married man, what's the one thing that you have had to change about yourself?"

I didn't know where to begin.

After thinking about it for about ten seconds, I jokingly said, "When you're married, and you're lying in bed with your wife, you can't just let one rip the way you do when you're around your guy friends watching a ball game."

This particular friend has since told me that the marital advice I gave him—even though it was said in jest—was some of the best advice he received, and after he got married, he quickly found out from his wife that she was not going to put up with his farting in her presence.

As a guy, you know that most guys under thirty (okay, maybe under forty) treat flatulence as an intramural sport. Guys compare the sound and smell of flatulence and even pay each other compliments such as, "Oh . . . that was a really good one." For some guys, a good fart is the highlight of their day—they are proud and tell their buddies about it and lament that they weren't around at the time he let the big one rip.

Virtually every guy I know has at one time or another participated in a makeshift contest with his buddies to see who can fart the loudest. Some guys I knew when I was younger would actually take pride in their ability to out-fart their friends (yes, it really is sick if you think about it).

Your wife, on the other hand, will not play this game. Like most women, she will probably find it revolting that we men tend to play this game on an all-too regular basis. I'm told the overwhelming majority of women do not fart like guys, and if they do, they will go to the nearest bathroom. Many women just don't get why we men pass gas at all.

Even though my mom taught us that farting was bad manners when we were kids, my brother Chris would make a game out of farting, much to the chagrin of our youngest brother, Kenny. When Chris knew that he was going to let one rip, he would tackle Kenny, sit on his head, and then fart on him. Of course, Dino, Chris, and I laughed while Kenny, with one hand over his nose, would slug Chris with his other hand and desperately try to free himself from the "gas chamber." We were quintessential boys being boys.

As kids, we were so bad that we—Chris usually was the instigator—would even let one or two rip in church. Have you even been around four young boys when one of them farts out loud in the middle of a priest's homily? Within seconds, all of us would be laughing almost uncontrollably. My poor mom, the stuff we put her through. Chris hasn't changed all that much. While he doesn't sit on Kenny's head anymore, when he farts his wife tells him that his stink "permeates the walls" in their house and that one day he's going to asphyxiate the family.

As a guy, you know the farting game doesn't end in your adolescence years. After graduating from college, I lived with three other guys in a two-bedroom apartment, thus, there were two of us to a bedroom. The bedrooms were separated by one paper-thin wall and if I was in one room I could hear even the faintest noise coming from the other, especially at night when I went to bed. One of my roommates took pride in keeping the other three of us awake by farting as loud as he could. After he let one rip, he would laugh and say something like, "That's nothing. Wait until the next one!" Thankfully, I didn't share a room with him, so I only had to deal with the noise.

I can't imagine four female roommates dealing with the same dynamic of unwanted bodily sounds.

Speaking from firsthand experience, once you get married, you will have to make a fairly dramatic change to your flatulence routine. Your wife won't accept the canned excuses that you have used around your buddies, such as "I just ate a bowl of extra spicy chili." And if you have a dog, you can only get away with blaming the pooch a couple of times before your wife catches on. You're just going to have to accept that you're not living with the boys anymore, and your wife will make that abundantly clear to you within a matter of seconds after you let one slip in her presence.

27.

The Good, the Bad, and the Ugly

"Bachelors know more about women
than married men; if they didn't,
they'd be married too."

—H. L. MENCKEN

Every so often, your wife will slap a label on you prefaced by these two simple words: "You are." Applying these labels isn't something she will do on an arbitrary basis—in most cases, she will be responding to something (usually it's something that will make her very happy or very mad) that you did or said that will elicit such a label.

These so-called labels will run the gamut from being highly complimentary to being somewhat offensive (although as a guy you probably won't be that offended—and remember, you deserve the label because of your actions or inaction). There is the rather wide range of "You are" labels for your wife to choose from, and I like to think of them as falling into one of three categories: the Good, the Bad, and the Ugly.

The tone in which your wife will deliver these labels will also vary greatly. The "Good" labels can be delivered in a warm, caring tone. The "Bad" labels can be delivered in a disappointing and disapproving tone. And the "Ugly" labels, well, they can be delivered by your wife with downright contempt and utter disbelief.

I informally polled several of my married guy friends and asked about the labels their wives slap on them, and here, to wit, are some of the more popular labels broken out by category:

The Good

○ You are such a wonderful husband.

○ You are so caring.

○ You are so sweet.

○ You are so romantic. (After a while, don't count on hearing this very often.)

○ You are such a good son.

○ You are such a great father.

○ You are so thoughtful. (As with "You are so romantic," don't count on hearing this very often.)

○ You are so generous.

○ You are such a good example.

○ You are so kind.

○ You are so sexy when you . . . (*fill in the blank*).

The Bad

o You are such a bad example!

o You are so juvenile!

o You are such a guy!

o You are so immature!

o You are more interested in sports than in me!

o You can be a real slob!

o You are so unromantic!

o You can be so lazy!

o You are too horny!

The Ugly

o You are being such a jerk!

o You are so selfish!

o You are such a poor role model!

o You are not the man I married!

o You are embarrassing me!

o You are impossible!

o You are really disgusting sometimes!

o You are exhaustingly childish!

o You are devoid of emotion!

o You are way too horny . . . and you're not getting any tonight!

The labels or declarations that fall under the Bad and the Ugly have exclamation points because, trust me, your wife will say them with much emphasis and very strong feelings (most likely shouting). The best way to cope with—and possibly avoid—the Bad and Ugly labels is simple: acquiesce to your wife. Remember the study I told you about by researchers at the University of Washington? Give in to your wife and you will both be happy. Now, if you do get slapped with Bad or Ugly labels by your wife, just remember, you probably did something pretty idiotic to drive her to that point.

28.

Not Quite Finished

"If you want your wife to listen to you, then
talk to another woman: she will be all ears."
—SIGMUND FREUD

Herewith are some topics that, while they are important in your education about women and marriage, don't require a separate chapter. Nonetheless, I want to make sure that I address these issues and provide you with some helpful advice.

Selecting a Wedding Date

When you are considering your wedding date with your fiancée, try to talk her into having your wedding in mid to late February or anytime in July. You may think that your wedding is only one night, but believe me, between the planning, meetings with the caterer and photographer, dinners, rehearsal, and the potential travel required for the ceremony and honeymoon, you will be highly susceptible to missing some key football, baseball, basketball, or hockey games, depending on the date you select. By February, the Super Bowl has just passed so football season is over and college basketball's NCAA tournament doesn't start until mid-March, which gives you enough time to catch the action once you return from your honeymoon. July should be obvious; the only semi-interesting thing going sports-wise in July is Major League Baseball's all-star game, which is no biggie to miss.

Her Friends

Even if you don't like them, you're going to have to accept them.

Your Rough-Around-the Edges Friend

Just about every guy has one: the friend who just can't help himself and says things that just about everyone else—especially women—finds offensive. While you may laugh at his jokes while bonding on the golf course, it's probably best to limit your wife's exposure to him to just a few times a year. You know he's eventually going to say and/or do something stupid that will piss off your wife, so don't ever try to defend him. Denounce his words and actions swiftly and repeatedly —"I can't believe what a jerk he was being." Your wife will find your "sense of mindfulness" surprisingly revealing and comforting.

Marry a Younger Woman

Not for the reason you think. Chances are, you will never be as mature a person as your wife. If you marry a woman who is roughly the same age as you, while biologically you are the same age, it's highly likely that she is and always will be a hell of a lot more mature than you. You know the saying, "Girls mature faster than boys"? Well, some guys I know have yet to fully mature mentally. My brother Chris, who is fifty-one going on seventeen, is seven years younger than his wife. So, in maturity years, she's about fifteen years his senior. My wife is four years younger than I am, but she is at least four years more mature than I am. If you marry a younger woman, you will able to somewhat close the gap in the maturity chasm that naturally exists between most men and women.

Doing Laundry

Once you start cohabitating with a woman, you can no longer wash all of the clothes in the hamper at the same time. Not only can you no longer wash all of the dirty clothes at the same time, believe it or not, not everything goes in the dryer. As usual, I'm speaking from firsthand experience; women's sweaters and bras tend to shrink and get damaged (sometimes permanently) when you put them in the "high heat" cycle in the dryer.

"You ruined it!" I used to hear those three words from my wife after I made the mistake of putting something of hers in the dryer that clearly said "hang dry" or "lay flat to dry" on the label that I neglected to read. When in doubt, take your wife's clothes to the drycleaner.

Controlling the Remote

Your TV remote control belongs in one of two places: your left hand or your right hand. Controlling the TV remote is a man's inalienable right. As a guy, you know that you don't necessarily care what's on; you want to know *what else* is on. Establish this immutable ground rule the day you move in with a woman.

Feng Shui, Feng Shmui

Feng Shui, I am told, is about "becoming aware of your environment and applying energetic principles to your surroundings." My wife has a Feng Shui book full of advice on how Feng Shui influences your life. For example, the book states, among other things, that "A chronically dirty stove can significantly alter your financial status." What a crock. I don't know one guy who buys the whole Feng Shui thing. Problem is, a lot of women—especially once they become home-owners—embrace Feng Shui principles when decorating their house.

A woman who is a supposed Feng Shui "expert" attended one of Lissette's parties and upon observing some things about our house, she told my wife three things: 1) the TV in the armoire at the foot of our bed creates "negative energy" absorbed by our feet, 2) the books in our bookcase are like daggers, and 3) the eight wood beams on the ceiling in our living room create downward pressure on anyone who sits under them and people should avoid sitting under them.

I asked my wife to never again invite this woman to her parties. Be prepared for the whole Feng Shui thing. You'll recognize it immediately because your wife will start rearranging the furniture in a way that will make no sense whatsoever to you.

When You Really Know You Screwed Up

Don't even try to justify it—just admit it as soon as you can and tell your wife that you're sorry.

Two Words

Two one-syllable words can save you a lot of grief. Those words are, "Yes dear." Use them. A lot.

A Final Word

When I finished writing this book, a few friends asked me why I didn't write a chapter on the touchy subject of sex and marriage. Listen, there are dozens of books out there written by sex counselors and couples therapists telling you how to keep the passion in your marriage and spice up your love life. You don't need me to weigh in on the subject. Plus, to be brutally honest, I had self-preservation in mind: had I even alluded to our sex life in this book, my wife would have disowned me.

Be that as it may, when it comes to the topic of sex and marriage, I am reminded of a joke that one of my married friends told me before I got married that perhaps best embodies the different points of view that some men and women have once the wedding rings go on.

Here's the joke:

A happy couple just got married, and the newlyweds are enjoying their wedding reception. The groom is standing by the bar wearing an ear-to-ear grin. His best man walks up to him, hands him a beer, and asks, "Why such a big smile?" Pointing to his bride across the room, the groom says, "You see that girl over there? Well, she just became my wife and now I can have sex every night of the week."

Meanwhile, the bride is sipping champagne and chatting with her maid of honor. "Want to know the thing I'm happiest about?" asks the bride. "Do tell!" says the maid of honor with great anticipation. Looking at her husband across the room, the bride says, "You see that guy over there? Well, he just became my husband, and now we only have to have sex once a week."

Hall Passes

There will be times when you need a break from your wife and when your wife needs a break from you. Look, people get on each other's nerves, and when you live under the same roof with someone 24/7 and face the daily pressures of work, family, and finances, or when one of your favorite teams is doing shitty, it's going to happen.

You know the saying, "Absence makes the heart grow fonder." Well, when you *desperately* need that break, just tell your wife you have been given a hall pass by yours truly (how could she possibly say no?). Cut along the dotted lines, present the hall pass to her, and plan your hall pass getaway with a buddy or two. You'll come back from your hall pass ready to take on the world—or something like that.

YOU EXHAUST ME

HALL
PASS
#1

YOU EXHAUST ME

HALL
PASS
#2

YOU EXHAUST ME

HALL
PASS
#3

YOU EXHAUST ME

HALL
PASS
#4

YOU EXHAUST ME

HALL
PASS
#5

YOU EXHAUST ME

HALL
PASS
#6

Acknowledgments

Doing something the first time always involves a learning curve and writing/publishing a book is no exception. This endeavor was quite a journey, and along the way there were several people I regularly called on.

I am grateful to The Book Couple, Carol and Gary Rosenberg, my editor and graphic designer. Please judge my book by its cover, as Gary's design is, in book-review vernacular, five stars. Carol took a decent manuscript and made it markedly better.

For my friend, Carol Chanel, who self-published long before I did, I am grateful for your endless enthusiasm and guidance.

A special thank you to Donna Flores, Michael Jensen, Gina Magee, Michelle McSkimming, Olga Mizrahi and Kathy Parsons.

Of course, *You Exhaust Me* would not have come to fruition without my wife, Lissette. Thank you for being my muse and inspiration, and biggest cheerleader. Finally, a big thank you to my beautiful daughters for always supporting and encouraging me.

About Lissette

If you were expecting an "About the Author" page at the end of this book, you haven't missed it. I first wanted to tell you about Lissette. After all, she is one of two central "characters" and without her this book wouldn't exist.

Lissette is passionate about many things, among them are: art, reading, theatre, travel (her travels have taken her to such destinations as Tibet, Cambodia, Indonesia, Cuba, Vietnam, Philippines and Sri Lanka), and volunteering in our community, where she is a board member of several local nonprofit organizations. Thanks to her, our house has distinct artwork from countries in every hemisphere.

With an undergraduate degree in Public Relations and completed Masters coursework in Spanish Linguistics and Literature, Lissette founded her own Hispanic Marketing and PR firm, and has created campaigns for a diverse roster of clients.

But, most important—at least to me—Lissette is the most amazingly gracious, caring and considerate person I have ever met. She is a wonderful wife, an incredible mother of our three daughters, and a big-time dog lover. She also has a great sense of humor and has the most positive outlook on life of anyone I've ever met.

About the Author

A New England native, Bob Marsocci resides in Southern California with his wife, three daughters, and two dogs. *You Exhaust Me* is his first book.

Bob can be reached at bmarsocci64@gmail.com.
Also visit www.bobmarsocci.com

Did you enjoy this book?

Many thanks for reading *You Exhaust Me.* If you enjoyed reading my book, I would be pumped if you would please post a positive review on Amazon. Thank you.

Made in the USA
San Bernardino, CA
13 August 2017